Single Again

Dating and Meeting New Friends the Second Time Around

George Blake

Adams Media Corporation
Holbrook, Massachusetts

Published by
Adams Media Corporation
260 Center Street, Holbrook, MA 02343. U.S.A.
www.adamsmedia.com

ISBN: 1-58062-280-1

Printed in Canada.

J I H G F E D C B A

Library of Congress cataloging-in-publication data available upon request from the publisher.

This publication is designed to provide accurate and authoritative information with regard to the subject matter covered. It is sold with the understanding that the publisher is not engaged in rendering legal, accounting, or other professional advice. If legal advice or other expert assistance is required, the services of a competent professional person should be sought.
— From a *Declaration of Principles* jointly adopted by a Committee of the American Bar Association and a Committee of Publishers and Associations

This book is available at quantity discounts for bulk purchases. For information, call 1-800-872-5627.

* * *

WARNING!!! READ THIS BOOK AT YOUR OWN RISK!!!

It may be hazardous to your single lifestyle and may cause you to get out and enjoy yourself in the company of other single people, possibly resulting in marriage and other good things.

* * *

THANKS TO . . .
Kathleen for the idea;
and to Marguerite and Kathleen for the assistance;
. . . and the thousands of singles who took the time
and effort to contribute their experiences and ideas,
for the well-being of all singles.
THANKS A BUNCH!

CONTENTS

Preface,
Or Why I Wrote This Book

WHEN I BECAME SINGLE after 18 years of marriage, I found that I was a fish out of water. My married friends seemed to desert me for most social functions, and I was beginning to feel like an outcast. I didn't know what to do, where to go, how and where to meet other single persons . . . and there was no one around to set me straight in my new singles environment.

I learned that most other singles were in my same predicament. That's when I recognized the need for research that would answer these and dozens more questions and problems second-time singles encounter every day, especially "new" second-time singles. And that's when I recognized the need for a book to report research findings, a book written by a single person who has experienced the single scene and written in terms the single person readily relates to.

So I began what turned out to be 14 years of research among over fifteen thousand people who became single again after a divorce or death of a spouse. I did my research not in laboratories or clinics or on couches (well . . . maybe a *few* couches) but at hundreds of singles parties, church-sponsored events, singles club functions, bars and lounges, dances, picnics, and so forth. I did my research just about anywhere single people were apt to show up.

But I did more than just research and interview people: I organized and sponsored more than a thousand singles parties, dances, and outings of all types. I ran 27 singles ocean cruises. I started or viii ✳ Single Again

promoted numerous singles organizations. And I wrote a popular "singles" column for several newspaper chains. In this book, I'll share some of the interesting experiences of the many readers of my column, as well as those of the thousands of other singles I met along the way.

BUT HOLD IT!

If you are searching for an "advice to the lovelorn" book, don't buy this one. It's not that kind of book.

And if you like a lot of psychological mumbo-jumbo, this book isn't for you either.

This book offers case histories and success (or failure) stories about problems and OPPORTUNITIES that inure to "second-time" singles in their everyday social lives. I've changed names and places, so no one can accuse me of spilling the beans on their secret lives, other than that, all the stories and events are true.

And while I do give a few suggestions and recommendations, they are based on what is *really* happening in the singles world, rather than on what people *wish* were happening or might *think* is happening. You'll see that I don't pull my punches and that I tell it like it is, so put on your thick skin, and jump right in.

To make the book livelier, I have interspersed stories and commentary with letters from some of the thousands of people who have written to me about their experiences as second-time singles.

With 50 million singles already in the market and an additional 5 million people joining the singles scene each year, there certainly should be a lot of people out there who will find this book a helpful shortcut to "jumpstart" the rest of their lives. At least I hope so.

So in answer to the question about why I wrote this book, it was largely motivated by a sense of wanting to help newly single people get off on the right foot and giving long-time singles some new ammunition to help improve their lifestyles.

And I might add that the thought of 50 million $ingle$ buying this book also crossed my mind.

✳ **1** ✳

It's a Jungle Out There

W E'RE NOT GETTING any younger!
That's why I'm so impatient with single people who are slow to change and adapt to the new single life in which they find themselves. That's why I don't beat around the bush but get right to the heart of the situation. I'm brutally honest, and this honesty and impatience can sometimes be misconstrued as male chauvinism. But nothing is farther from the truth.

There are many millions more adult single women than adult single men, and it has been my experience that the majority of single women are much slower than men to accept the fact that they are now single again. Things can be very different for them—and sometimes very difficult for them—the second time around, and I want to help them get through the difficult periods. I get impatient and antsy at the slow pace of some of these women to accept their new status, and it may show from time to time. Please bear with me. Maybe I need to pray for patience.

LORD, GIVE ME PATIENCE!

BUT I WANT IT RIGHT NOW!

In my university days, I don't recall any psychological courses directed toward single life or singles' problems. The courses I studied seldom if ever even acknowledged that singles might have any problems. And the high-powered psychologists on TV and in the newspapers are usually happily married people who, when they give us singles advice, simply dress up their "marrieds" advice in "singles" clothing. That won't work! We singles have distinct problems (and opportunities) that require special attention and sometimes involve complex solutions.

Some people's problems are part of their own personalities, and no one can help them except themselves. People who are rude, pushy, negative, conceited, battle axes, pains in the rears, etc., etc., can only change by changing themselves and changing their outlooks on life. They'll recognize their personality traits—or shortcomings—as they read on, and I hope they will want to modify them so that they'll better fit into today's singles society. If they don't, they're "goners."

One of the major problems in single life is that of loneliness. Here the media psychologists can describe how loneliness *acts* on your psyche, but they don't usually have *practical* answers about how to *eliminate* loneliness from your life. Single people don't need to be told how loneliness can affect them; they already know this better than anyone. What they need is to learn the best ways to *overcome* loneliness . . . and I hope that's where I can help. The loneliness problem *can* be solved with a little effort, as you'll see as you read on.

And even though I might sound jocular in many of my comments, you should know that I take very seriously that getting along in the singles world as a new single person may very well be the most important thing you'll ever do for yourself.

The greatest joys I have ever experienced have come as a result of people who followed my recommendations and successfully got out of their ruts. Here is one example from one of my readers:

✳ **Dear George:**
I read your column all the time. I'm a widow and have been so lonely in my new city (I moved here 6 months ago), and I only had one friend. I finally took your advice and embarked on a 7-day Caribbean cruise for singles.

I met so many nice people from my area that I now have SIX good friends, and I'm not lonely anymore. I'm dancing, socializing, getting out, and enjoying myself as never before.

You are the cause of this, and I will thank you for the rest of my (happy) life.

When I received this letter, I framed it and hung it on the wall above my word processor. It made everything that I have tried to do suddenly seem important and worthwhile. And that brings me back to my "impatience." I wish every single person would do as this reader did, and as quickly as possible. Get out and socialize. Bury your preconceived Victorian notions. Take the bull by the horns and get off your duff. Get out into the world!

Here's what happened to another reader who followed my suggestions:

✳ Dear George:

I am a 44-year-old attractive divorced female. I thought I would look and feel "cheap" if I went to a singles party or dance, and I was fiercely determined never to stoop so low as to go to one. But, finally, my loneliness and the persistence of your urgings in your newspaper column induced me to go to a singles activity one evening. It took all the courage I could muster.

As it turned out, no one thought I was "cheap," and, in fact, hardly anyone even noticed me at all. I thought I would stand out in the crowd as a newcomer (or worse, a brazen man hunter) and that everyone would stare. But like everything else, it too was a figment of my imagination. No one treated me rudely or with any disrespect. I was left free to do what I wanted and to talk to whomever I pleased, with no hassles.

I hate to admit it, but I found the singles atmosphere less intimidating than all the parties I attended with my husband when we were married. Thanks to you, George, I'm getting my act together and getting out again. Spread the word to other women who are wasting their time alone. God bless you!

To people like this reader, the singles scene was dreadful and foreboding until they decided to check it out for themselves. And that's the best advice I can give you. Don't rely on rumors. Don't let "marrieds" tell you what's going on in the singles world. And for goodness sake, don't listen to all the bunk that is dished out by the television and newspapers about the poor plight of single people. Check out the local singles scene on your own. See for yourself what *really* goes on. In the *vast majority* of cases, you'll be pleasantly surprised.

Many who took my suggestions have found the OPPORTUNITY to enjoy a really fulfilling life as a single man or woman once again. They gave themselves a second chance, so to speak, to restart their lives. They attacked this new challenge with vigor and enthusiasm. They're my kind of people.

The singles scene need not be scary or dreadful any more than being married should be. And just as it's true that all marriages and all married people aren't good or happy, so too all single people and all singles events aren't 100 percent good. You are going to run into a few bad apples whatever your lifestyle. So when you do encounter a bad one, don't get discouraged. *It's the exception.* Move on!

The singles scene has been unfairly portrayed by various individuals as a low-class, desperate way of life. That's rubbish! These naysayers seem to pick out one or two instances of singles with problems and then milk them to death for years on end until we come to believe that these problems coexist with single life. It's a lot of baloney!

A major problem with the singles scene is the lopsided ratio of single women to single men, which I mentioned earlier. Except for five sparsely populated states in the USA, single women outnumber single men in every state in the union (and most Canadian provinces) by wide margins. In some metropolitan markets, adult single women outnumber their male counterparts by as much as *10 to one*! And that's where you'll find what I call the "singles jungle": women fighting for dates; women fighting for affection; women fighting for male attention. And this problem begets another problem: Some single men who suddenly realize they are "in demand" tend to become overconfident, overbearing, and downright conceited (even though some of them, if the ratios were reversed, probably couldn't get a date in a hundred years, even with a "fistful of fifties"). These men become the "jack-asses" of the jungle. You'll recognize them when you see them.

I describe these and many other "inhabitants" of the jungle on the succeeding pages. And guess what? Someplace in this book you are likely to find a description of *yourself*. Whether or not you like this description and whether or not you want to change what you see remains your decision. But most of you ARE included in this book.

Isn't it nice being a celebrity?

You've Got to Be Creative!

In the singles jungle, it's survival of the "fittest," and often the fittest are those who are the most creative. You'll get a lot of creative ideas as you read on, but I just had to highlight this one creative woman from an Illinois suburb. She came up with a very creative idea on how to meet successful bachelors.

Her brother happened to own a classic 1962 Corvette sports car, which he let her "borrow" for her creative experiment. She placed a classified ad in the "Classic Cars for Sale" section in her local newspaper. She listed her brother's classic Corvette for sale to the best offer and described it generously. She received 51 calls to her ad, and as she suspected, most just happened to be successful single men . . . the kind who had sufficient disposable income to be able to afford a classic such as this. Of course, they all wanted to look at the car, and as they inspected it, she inspected them. It was a great conversation starter, and seven of the men ended up asking her for a date.

And, as she knew would be the case, none of them made an "acceptable" offer on her brother's Corvette (which he didn't want to sell anyway). But she got a lot of "mileage" from the Corvette, without ever taking it out of the driveway.

If you're going to be king or queen of the jungle and want to meet the cream of the crop, a little creativity goes a long way.

✳ 2 ✳

Women First Through the Wringer

ADJUSTING BACK INTO single life can be a real problem for many women. And it continues to get worse every year for those who waste their early single years moping around or refusing to acknowledge they are now part of the singles scene. Like it or not, ladies, take it from a friend: Get into your new singles environment as soon as humanly possible. If you don't have someone to accompany you, then do it by yourself. Don't sit there in front of the boob tube and vegetate. That's wasting a good human being—you!

As I mentioned previously, in the singles world, many of us tend to create our own problems because of our attitudes. I would say the biggest contributor to a lot of single women's unhappiness is their *attitude*. Their attitude toward life, toward their fellow singles, toward society, toward other women, toward men, toward just about everything they can criticize, condemn, and complain about. I've seen attractive women turn off men in droves with their complaining or negative attitudes.

Try to look at the positive side of life. If you search out what is *right* about things rather than what is *wrong* with them, I guarantee your single life will improve dramatically. This is the most important suggestion you'll get out of this book. If you have an attitude problem, change your attitude, and you'll change your life . . . for the better.

Here's another big problem. Many of the newly single women I have talked with think they have to revert back to the days before they were married (no matter how long ago that might have been) to a time when they were popular with the boys or may have been the queen of the ball, with men fighting for their attention or affection. These women (my guess is 50 percent of newly single women) seem to think that things will revert back to the way they were before their marriages. But what a shock they're in for! And the shock gets worse as the women age. (Remember, I said I'd be truthful!)

The newly single woman has usually put on a few years, and probably a few extra pounds and miscellaneous blemishes and sags. She might even have a few youngsters at home (a definite roadblock in the dating/mating world, especially if your ex lives nearby). If you put them all together, they spell LESS DESIRABLE THAN BEFORE! Like everything else, women change over the years, and if they are going to be well-adjusted single women, they must accept the fact that things have changed and *can never be the same as they were in her pre-marital days*. The average newly single woman may find very few GOOD single men fighting for her attention and affection. In fact, she may wind up fighting for THEIRS. (Wash my mouth out with soap!)

Many newly divorced women become cynical about a relationship with men. They mistrust every man's intentions and usually put down men the first chance they get. This attitude is often brought about as a result of her ex-husband and his attorney trying to rob her of everything during their divorce proceedings.

The women who walk around with this chip on their shoulders had better get rid of it pronto. *We men insist on being judged by our own actions*, not on someone else's, especially if that someone else is an ex-husband. This type of "chip" is easily recognized by most men, and avoided like the plague.

Forget your divorce proceedings and all the gory details that led up to it. Every man is different, just as every woman is. Judge us as WE are.

Here's another problem many newly single women find hard to deal and cope with: women's liberation! With women's lib a permanent fixture on today's social scene, some of the customs, mores, and actions that were unthinkable a decade or two ago are considered normal behavior today—things like calling a man on the telephone, asking a man for a dance or a date, paying your own way (or even paying for his), driving yourself to a date, entering lounges alone, and going to singles parties and dances by yourself. I could go on and on, but you get the point. Women's liberation made it a different world out there, and you'd better accept the fact and learn to blend in.

The singles scene can be a very pleasant journey toward an interesting and rewarding period in your life, if you don't allow your "attitude" to erect a barricade.

An ancient Chinese philosopher once said, "Every great journey begins with the first step." For many women in today's single world, that one step can be the most difficult action they can imagine. But once most of them take that step and see that everything is still all right with them, they quickly take their places in the singles world and eagerly anticipate each new day. I've seen it happen hundreds and hundreds of times. Try it. You'll like it.

3

Men's Turn in the Barrel

T HE "SINGLE" MALE SPECIES appears to have more distinct differences than single females. These differences are especially noticeable when it comes to personality comparisons between men who are divorced and those who are widowers.

The widower who first ventures into the singles scene often becomes the hapless prey of aggressive women just waiting to spring the trap. I've seen many of these men blindly stumble into a relationship—and marriage—with someone they hardly knew. Just because they had been married practically all their adult lives, they felt uncomfortable without it.

Here's a letter I received from a widower that says it all:

Dear George:

My wife passed away 2 years ago after 27 years of marriage. I was so lonely for someone to talk to every night that before I realized it, I had remarried. And I might add that I remarried without really knowing much about my new partner. Now that we have lived together for about a year, we realize too late that we don't have anything in common, and, unfortunately, we get on each other's nerves.

We are parting gracefully, but everything is in such turmoil that I wish I had known from the start to become acquainted with more single women so that I could have made a more rational decision. Maybe if you print this letter, other widowers will be warned not to jump into the first dating situation that presents itself but to look around and date a number of women to be sure of making the right decision. In my haste to find another "friend" like I had in my original marriage, I only found trouble. I was better off being lonely.

Unfortunately, I know a number of widowers who suffered this same sad experience. And the thing that hurts the most is that these guys are really good people who would be loyal husbands and great companions to a new wife. But they all selected the first gal and jumped into a hasty marriage or relationship.

Some women know about this tendency of new widowers to latch onto the first friendly face that comes along, and they try to make sure they are that first "friendly face." One widower told me that more than a dozen women—all strangers—called him after his wife's funeral, inviting him to dinner. It seems that there are women who read the obituary pages of the local newspaper, and when they see there is a male survivor somewhere around the age group they are seeking, they set up a campaign to nail him. They wait a respectable time—like about 2 days after the funeral—and then spring their traps.

That same widower encountered women who even attended the wakes to meet or look over the surviving male, posing as friends of the deceased wife (who, by the way, isn't around to dispute that friendship). The next thing you know, we'll have to fight off these "widower spiders" at the deathbeds of sick wives.

But they all seem to know what they're doing, because in many cases, the new widower is easily led down the primrose path to the altar. It is my observation that *nearly half* of newly widowed men are putty in the hands of aggressive females and, not knowing what to do in the situation, follow her dictates. And in most cases, their lives with the new aggressive females who snagged them are more like a prison sentence.

Follow the advice of this letter writer, men, and get to know several great women before you settle on the best one.

Here's another thing that bugs me about some widowers (and widows too)—those usually over 50 years of age who get remarried. Many of them are so worried about whether or not the heirs in their own family are going to get *all* of *their* money that they treat their new marriage partners as a *drain on their heir's inheritance.* I have seen this in nearly half of every remarriage of widows and widowers. They are more interested in what they are going to leave their heirs than they are in having a wonderful second life with their new spouses.

And every one of these people explains it by saying that they think this way because their family is blood-related and the new spouse is an "accommodation" or a latecomer, or something else that makes the new spouse sound and feel like an interloper or, at best, a second-class citizen.

I have even known some remarried people who pay their own lunch and dinner checks apart from their spouse, even though they live and eat together every day. Can you believe it?

If you are in your later years and you are lucky enough to find someone to love you despite your infirmities or age or whatever, I think you should treat that person as you would like to be treated. And don't make them feel like they aren't appreciated or needed . . . because they are needed far more than a few bucks are.

And don't be afraid to leave your new spouse some big bucks if you depart this world first. After all, your spouse put up with your crankiness in your old age on a daily basis. Your kids didn't!

Now let's examine the newly *divorced* male. It is my opinion, after observing thousands of these men, that half of them fall into one of these four categories:

TYPE I—THE LOVER. This newly single male feels that the first thing he must do is go out and prove to all the world that he is really a very desirable, very masculine stud. He'll probably try to date everything with a skirt on (or off). He'll tend to be boisterous, loud, and unnecessarily outgoing, to the point of being obnoxiously extroverted. He's going to show the world what his ex-spouse is missing and the mistake she made in not raising him to his "rightful" position of sainthood during their marriage.

Unfortunately, TYPE I males don't come off as desirable or masculine but instead as crashing bores to be avoided at all costs. Whenever we meet TYPE I males, we all in our hearts secretly give his ex-wife a round of applause for having the good sense to leave him.

TYPE II—THE LOAFER. This man, after years of being harnessed to the marital plow, goes off the deep end to show how casual, uncaring, uncouth, and undependable he can be. It's sort of as if it's a new life for him and he's rebelling against the way he has lived for the past umpteen years of married life. Unfortunately, his new attitude is self-defeating in most cases, because women today—as before—still want and appreciate a stable, dependable, caring, couth male. The TYPE II male usually quickly runs through the list of available women like the proverbial "you know what" through a tin horn, and ends up unloved and unwanted.

TYPE III—THE LOATHER. This guy got a bum deal from his ex-wife, to hear him tell it. He doesn't trust women, hates them all, and treats them like dirt. Courtesy, respect, and concern for women's feelings have gone out the window. TYPE IIIs can be very troublesome—even dangerous—and should be avoided.

TYPE IV—THE LOSER. You could also call him the "wimp" even though he might be a champion prizefighter, football tackle, or president of a major corporation. He comes out of his marriage as meek as a lamb awaiting the slaughter. He's a sitting duck for the first aggressive woman who latches on to him. TYPE IVs usually let the woman lead them around by the nose, and they seem resigned to it. They've lost their spark and *joi de vivre*. They're usually engaged 6 months after their divorce, in what turns out to be a total mismatch. Luckily, TYPE IVs usually snap out of it, though it may take several years.

It sounds like a contradiction, but while women MUST NOT think they can revert back to the way things were before they were married, these men, on the other hand, MUST revert back to their premarital ways if they hope to find lasting companionship in their lives.

✳ **4** ✳

Meeting Other Singles

PROBABLY THE MOST ASKED QUESTION among singles is, Where is the best place to meet other singles? Of the thousands of questions I have fielded throughout the years, this one accounts for about 70 percent of them.

The answer—a simple one—is, EVERYWHERE!

With the divorce rate and the death rate ending millions of marriages every year, it's almost as easy to meet singles as it is to meet marrieds; they're all over the place. But many singles have their heads buried in the sand and wouldn't recognize another single person if they jumped up and bit them (which, when you think of it, isn't such a bad idea. It's called a hickey).

Or we have those singles with tunnel vision, who *indirectly* pass up plenty of opportunities to meet other singles. What do I mean by meeting singles indirectly? Here's an example of what happened at one of my singles parties that may explain it. I've seen this same type of thing happen dozens of times.

A lady (I'll call her Sally) was hell-bent on finding a man at all costs. She was attractive enough, but too overly aggressive, and she had tunnel vision. To her, it was "find a man at all costs." At my party, she had been talking to another woman when she spotted two men chatting together. Ignoring (and maybe insulting) the woman she had been talking to, she made a beeline for the men and struck up a conversation with them, really trying to impress them. Overly so! As it turned out, neither man asked Sally out, and she was left more frantic and frustrated than before. What she didn't know was that the lady she had brushed off had an eligible male cousin and also had two good bachelors in her office, either one of whom she would have been happy to introduce to Sally. And if Sally had given the woman more time, she would have learned that she was planning a house party for single friends and would have been happy to invite Sally—but not after getting the brush off. Sally blew it with her tunnel vision.

This is a good example of the indirect method of meeting other singles. Make good friends with lots of other people—male and female—because you never know who is in a position to introduce you to relatives, coworkers, sports partners, and so forth. Cast your bread upon the waters, and it will be returned to you tenfold. (As I write this, Sally is still shopping around for a man—and probably still screwing up the "indirect" way to meet him.)

If you are searching for a mate, a partner, or just a companion, don't ignore the everyday folks you encounter every day. They may turn out to be gold mines, as sources of new acquaintances for you, and they can make it easier, too, since they'll handle the sticky problem of introductions.

This indirect method works the same for males and females. ANYONE can be the source of your meeting Mr. or Ms. Wonderful. So if tunnel vision is your problem, try to overcome it now and become *sincere* friends with lots more people . . . and watch what happens.

The other way, of course, to meet new people is the direct way. In the direct way, you either meet other singles through introductions by mutual friends, or you introduce yourself to a stranger you want to get to know better.

✳ **Dear George:**
I have read what you say about indirectly meeting other singles, and I understand it. The problem I have is meeting women directly. I seem to say dumb things to new women, and they act like I'm some

kind of dope. I try not to come on strong, but I wind up coming on too
weak. Any hints for great opening lines?

Most of us use a pretty nerdy opening line with a strange girl, for example, "Hi! My name is Mortimer. What's yours?" It's rather blah, but it gets the job done in most cases.

However, one of my male readers sent me an opening line that he says is SUPERB! He claims it works 100 percent of the time to become instant friends with any woman you want. And he claims to use it everywhere—parties, dances, offices, supermarkets, airplanes.

He says that it gets him immediate attention, since the woman runs the gamut of feelings in a split second, from irritation to confusion, chagrin, perplexity, pathos, relief, thankfulness, friendship, appreciation . . . even love.

Wow! That has to be some opening line to accomplish all that, so I'll pass it on to all you male readers to try out.

But first of all, will the ladies please leave? The remainder of this chapter is for men only so that we don't tip our hand to women. Ladies, please stop now and go to the next chapter. This is for the guys. Go ahead, gals! Turn the page.

Okay, men! The gals are gone!

This reader's opening line that he claims is so great goes like this. You approach a single girl at a party (or office, or anywhere) and say, with a straight face:

"Pardon me miss, but aren't you a little embarrassed
being here tonight?"

He says she'll immediately become confused. She'll ponder: Is this a bad place to be? Is her dress ripped in the back? Does she have a piece of toilet paper stuck to the bottom of her shoe? Why should she be so embarrassed? What's wrong?

So she'll ask rather indignantly . . . even angrily:

"Why should I be embarrassed?"

He says that all women respond in exactly the same way. And at least she has started a two-way conversation. He answers her with the same straight face and serious tone:

**"Oh! I thought it might be embarrassing
being the prettiest girl at this party!
Doesn't that embarrass you just a little bit?"**

This reader claims that any walls of resistance she might have built up immediately come tumbling down. She'll burst into a smile, touch his arm or shoulder (instant touching), and thank him profusely for such a (novel) compliment. Usually, she's so relieved at not having something to be embarrassed about that she actually begins to appreciate him at once. From that point on, conversation between the two flows smoothly.

It seemed harmless enough, so guess what? I decided to try his suggestion one weekend when I attended two singles parties. I tried it on five women, and everything he claimed came true. What's more, the women seemed to get a big kick out of this novel way of complimenting them and meeting them at the same time.

Whatever opening line you use when you meet people directly, remember one thing: First impressions are lasting. If you can't say something pleasant or interesting at the outset, you're better off not speaking at all. Wait for her to start the conversation.

Now, let's get back and join the ladies on the next page.

✳ **5** ✳

Meeting at Singles Parties and Dances

SINGLES PARTIES AND DANCES are without a doubt the best places to meet your Mr. or Ms. Wonderful or just new single friends. Nearly everyone in attendance is there for one of two reasons: either to make new single acquaintances or to renew acquaintances with singles they already know. But the entire accent is on "meeting" and on "singles," so these types of events are your *best source* of making new friends. Now the only thing that's left is for some people to get up the *courage* to attend these parties.

✳ **Dear George:**

When I read your last newspaper column in which you bawled out us singles for not supporting more singles activities, I felt you were talking to me. I'm 42 years old and divorced for 2 years. I just don't feel single.

I did go to one singles happy hour at a prominent lounge, but I got so nervous by the time I got there that I couldn't open the door and instead turned around and went home.

I can't find other single women who aren't afraid to go either. I feel like I'm stuck in limbo.

Going to singles parties and activities is like getting olives out of a bottle. The first one is the hardest of all, and the rest come easier. If it'll help, belt down a double scotch first.

Here's how to overcome this "first time" fear. Get two or three women or men to accompany you the first time. They can be your relatives or neighbors or fellow workers, and they don't even have to be single. You can go with a married couple as support; the main thing is to go with someone you know whom you can lean on. After you've been to the party awhile and begin to feel at ease, move around on your own and notice what's going on and watch or listen to what the other guests are doing or saying. Chances are, depending on the type of party, everyone else is either dancing or conversing, or both. You've still got your friends to return to as your "crutch" in case you have an anxiety attack, so move around the party on your own and become relaxed.

Sometimes I get the feeling that people (especially women) think singles parties and activities are nothing more than wanton sex orgies where women are devastated by leering, lecherous men as soon as they enter. Maybe there are those types of parties; if so, I wouldn't blame anyone for avoiding them. But in all the hundreds of singles parties that I have either run or attended, I can honestly say that I wouldn't hesitate to bring my mother to any of them (except for the fact that she's married and my dad would give me hell).

✳ **Dear George:**

I have been single since my husband died 2 years ago, and I am shy about getting around men because I was married when I was 18. We were married over 45 years, and I'm so lonely. I would go to some singles parties, but I don't want to appear to be man hunting. I am only seeking companionship.

I will try to find courage to go to a singles event. I don't dance but am willing to learn. Should I take some dancing lessons? Please advise.

You can have just as nice a time at a singles party by meeting other *women* with whom you can share hobbies and interests . . . and companionship. And no one in his or her right mind at a singles party would look at you as being a man hunter, as you call it.

As far as dancing, it would be a good idea to learn some of the basic steps . . . but, here again, a lady friend can teach you these in a few minutes. However, if you do decide to take dancing lessons at a professional studio, beware of the dance instructor "charming" you into buying more lessons than Ginger Rogers ever had. Only spend what you can reasonably afford.

Not to get off the subject of singles parties, but this letter reminds me of another letter I received from a woman who took dancing lessons from a real "sharpie."

✳ **Dear George:**

I thought you'd be interested in an experience I had taking dancing lessons. I went to (bleep) dance studio, and my instructor was very charming. He sure did talk me into buying $3,000 worth of dance lessons. He said that he was going to make a beautiful dancer out of me and that we were going to be a dancing couple. Have your readers beware of dancing schools. I have quit the school. And I'm not a beautiful dancer.

I heard from another woman who got "romanced" into buying over $10,000 worth of dancing lessons. Wow! That's $5,000 a foot.

Before signing up for lessons, it's best to check references from previous students and the Better Business Bureau. It's much better to be a poor dancer than to be poor. But back to the singles parties.

✳ **Dear George:**

I recently moved back into town, and I'm determined not to fall into the doldrums trap of boring routines this year. I'm at loose ends as to what to do with my time and life. If you think singles get-togethers would welcome a vibrant, 55-year-young woman with wide business, social, cultural, and political interests, I might like to try them.

It has been my philosophy that everyone who attends a singles party or event should attend with the idea of what they can contribute to the party rather than what they can take from the party. In this way, we all become "givers," and everyone wins. You sound like you could contribute a lot, and I'm sure you would be most welcome from the first minute.

But a word of caution: At your first party, be observant and keep a lot of your experiences—and your opinions—to yourself. Look and listen until you become acquainted with a number of people. Don't start off as a person who knows it all and wants everyone to know it. You'll get plenty of time to discuss your wide range of interests at other parties . . . like maybe the third or fourth one.

✳ **Dear George:**

How can we be sure that the men we meet at singles parties are respectable and trustworthy?

You can't! Not until you get to know the people in attendance over a period of time. But that's the same with married parties, too, isn't it? Maybe even more so.

We all know that one or two "weirdos" will always manage to slip into just about any party ever given, whether singles or marrieds parties. I personally know of some very restricted church singles parties, very sedate and very solemn, that were attended by the worst "creeps" in town. And the same thing with private parties in homes, private clubs, art galleries, and so on. In other words, weirdos are here to stay; there is no way to completely eliminate them from attending any parties they want to attend because no one instantly recognizes them as being "strange" until it's too late.

I suggest you follow these simple rules when meeting a man for the first time, whether in church, a lounge, a private home, or anywhere:

Don't give out your last name to a stranger unless you know it's all right. (This prevents him from looking up your phone number in the directory and bothering you on the phone, or stopping by your home when you least expect him.) And, of course, it naturally follows: Don't give out your address or phone number unless you get to know him **very well**.

Don't let a new male acquaintance walk you to your car alone.

If a new male acquaintance asks you for a date and you want to date him, tell him you'll have to confirm it with him later, after you check your calendar, and ask him for HIS phone number and address. If he doesn't have a telephone or his local address is a nearby motel, MOVE ON!

On your first date, meet him in a public place and drive your own car or take a taxi. This way, if things don't work out, you always have transportation home.

Don't be snowed because he's a good dancer. Pay attention to everything else about him. Some of the biggest con artists are the best dancers. Conversely, some of the nicest guys are the lousiest dancers (for example, former President George Bush). Contrary to popular feminine opinion, *dancing isn't everything.*

I know of a woman who made arrangements to meet a man for a first date in a public restaurant; she drove her own car. As it turned out, after one drink, he became totally obnoxious and started to make passes at her. He let her know in no uncertain terms that bed would follow dessert. She excused herself between the salad and the main course to go to the ladies room. Instead, she made a beeline for her car, and drove home. She wouldn't have been able to escape as easily if she had depended on her new date for transportation.

It's smart to plan ahead.

✳ **Dear George:**

What can you say to a man, as your opening line (one full of wit and charm, of course) when mingling at a singles party, that has nothing to do with the weather?

Basically, it appears that many women are too nervous at the thought of even striking up a conversation with a strange man in the first place, so wit and charm aren't all that necessary. INTESTINAL FORTITUDE is the prime necessity. But as far as opening lines are concerned, I researched what women really do say to start a conversation with a strange man at parties, dances, cocktail lounge parties, and happy hours, and here are the best I heard. Judge for yourself which ones fit your personality.

"I love your jacket (or tie). What material is it made from?"

"I couldn't help noticing your ring (or wristwatch). There aren't many like it, are there?"

"I like your beard (or mustache). Does it get warm in summer?"

"I read about a singles cruise to the Caribbean. Have you ever been on a singles cruise?"

"Didn't I meet you recently at another party? My name is _____. What's yours?"

"This is a nice party, don't you think?"

One thing is certain. You'll have much better luck with a positive statement than a negative one. Women who start their conversations with a gripe or complaint will almost never get to first base with a man. After all, who wants to have a conversation with someone whose first impression is that she's an unhappy complainer?

The opening lines that worked best were those that started with a sincere compliment, followed by a question concerning the other person's interests. Those seemed to be the best for getting the conversation off and running.

Even though the vast majority of letters I receive are from women inquiring about meeting men, men can still follow these same tips when trying to meet women. Give a sincere compliment followed by a question. But be sure the question isn't suggestive or doesn't make you look like you're coming on too strong, as it will probably turn her off. We men have to be much more guarded about what we say to a strange woman so that we don't scare her away.

✳ 6 ✳

Meeting in Bars, in Lounges, and at Church-Sponsored Events

O NE MIGHT ASK, "Why in the world would he group the bar scene with church-sponsored events?"

The answer is a simple one. If I had divided both subjects into separate chapters, one or the other groups of readers would have passed up one of the chapters. And I think both of these subjects should be read by all singles—because after singles parties, these are very likely the best places to meet your Mr. or Ms. Wonderful.

I can already hear some of you scoffing. You're saying that either you'd never want to date a person you met in a bar or that church events are too boring. However, my research has proven beyond a doubt that after private singles parties and dances, these are the two primary places where singles meet. Read on!

✳ Dear George:

Where is a good place to meet nice men? I've heard that the bar scene is not where it's at. Where can a woman go?

If you want to meet men, *you've got to go where they are!* Oftentimes, that happens to be in a lounge. You've got to play by their rules if you are seriously searching for Mr. Wonderful. And women going into a lounge is not such a big deal anymore (except in women's own minds).

With women's liberation here to stay, it is very common to see today's modern woman stop for a relaxing drink after a hard day's work . . . and why shouldn't she? Men do! Aren't women entitled to partake of the same pleasures and pastimes? I personally know hundreds of nice, respectable, proper women who often stop at a lounge for a brief respite, any one of whom I would be proud to bring home to mother.

And I also know hundreds of good looking, respectable, reputable businessmen who regularly frequent lounges, many who go there for one main reason: It's the only place they know of to look for *their* Ms. Wonderful. When you stop and think about it, there probably is no better place, on a day-to-day basis, to make a lot of new single acquaintances than a *quality* lounge. These new acquaintances can usually lead to invitations to house parties, sports outings, and other good things. But the original meeting in many cases takes place in a nice, quality lounge.

Now, I'm not trying to make alcoholics out of the singles world, because you can drink fruit juices, soda pop, and plenty of other drinks that are nonalcoholic. Just do your own thing.

And I'm not talking about the bars that have the wet T-shirt contests or the free ladies night promotions. These places seem to draw the leering goons who think that every woman who walks in the door is fair prey. I'm talking about upscale lounges populated by upscale people. And to be an upscale person doesn't mean that you are filthy rich. It means that you are well mannered, couth, considerate of others' feelings, sociable, and friendly. If you fit this description, you'll feel comfortable in any upscale lounge.

When you try out a nice lounge, don't expect to hit paydirt on the first visit. Don't be in a big rush to meet ANY man. You've gone this long; a little longer isn't going to hurt. It takes time and patience. Don't get discouraged if the first man you meet doesn't turn out to be Mr. Right. Keep trying. As the old saying goes, "You've got to kiss a lot of frogs before you find your Prince Charming." At least you're in the right hunting grounds.

Pick out what appears to be a pleasant "business person's" type of lounge. That means one near large downtown office buildings, or one near a suburban office complex, or one on a busy street normally traveled by working people on their way home from the office. Just put your own common sense to work, and you'll find a place that you will like, as well as one that an upscale person with similar tastes to yours would like. And, of course, I'm talking about visiting the lounge during the *evening* happy hour or late evening . . . not the morning or afternoon hours. Otherwise your Mr. Wonderful might turn out to be Mr. Lush.

✳ **Dear George:**

I still can't get up enough nerve to go to a singles party or happy hour in a bar or lounge. Isn't there some other place for us shy ladies to gather?

How about a convent? I get your same comments all the time, and I still say that the first time you attend is the most difficult. Once you see that everyone else is the same as you are—all in the same boat—you'll quickly become at ease, and the rest of the visits you make will be duck soup. I've seen it proven over and over.

I've also heard a number of women (and some men) say, "I don't do the bar scene," or "I'd never want to meet a man (or woman) in a bar." I say BUNK! Granted, the so-called "singles bars" were pretty hokey, but they're on their way out of style, and I say good riddance to them. But there are tens of thousands of neighborhood lounges, businesspersons' lounges, and other quality-type lounges that are excellent places to frequent . . . especially during happy hour.

If the lounge serves hors d'oeuvres, so much the better. Bachelors who are tired of restaurant food and don't like to cook (and the silent majority of us bachelors don't like to cook our own meals) will often get much of their sustenance and variety at the hors d'oeuvres table. I call it a "bachelor buffet." It's the sociable way to get some food into us without the boring, long drawn-out routine in a restaurant (where, by the way, we already eat five or six hundred breakfasts and lunches every year). It's a pleasant change from the humdrum of eating alone.

Happy hour usually runs from 5:00 P.M. to 7:00 P.M., Monday through Friday. I personally have met more than a hundred wonderful women at these bachelor buffets, and I know of many women who have met just about as many men.

People who regularly stop at a particular lounge on their way home from work soon became a "familiar face" in the establishment and will find themselves striking up conversations with other "familiar faces." And that's the thing that good relationship-starts are made of.

A word of advice for the women reading this: Be calm! I've seen many women sheepishly enter a lounge, nervously scan the crowd for 2 seconds, and then hightail it out of there like a scared rabbit. I guess they are really just plain frightened, and that's too bad. Come in ladies and join the party. But don't creep in. Enter as the welcome guest you really are.

I recall once being in a lounge after work during a Friday happy hour. I was sitting at a table with several locally prominent businessmen when a woman—about 35 years old—poked her head in the door very nervously, scanned the lounge for no more than 3 seconds, and then hurriedly departed. It just so happened that this lounge was owned by a good friend of mine, and I didn't want to see him lose any business, so I chased after the woman and asked her why she had left so quickly. She answered that she was totally nervous about going into the lounge in the first place and, since she didn't see anyone she knew, she was going home. I told her that with the small amount of time she spent peering in the doorway, her whole family could have been sitting there and she wouldn't have spotted them. I introduced myself and insisted that she join me and my friends for a beverage. I suggested that it would calm her down and make her feel more at ease. I practically had to drag her inside, but she finally agreed.

I introduced her to my table guests and ordered her a beverage. As it turned out, she had had some business dealings with one of the guests at my table, and they both had a number of mutual friends. She soon became relaxed as they chatted merrily along.

I next introduced her to the owner of the lounge, the cocktail waitresses . . . and just about everyone I could think of. I made her feel at home as best I could. From that day on, she has felt completely at ease and returned nearly every Friday after work (and maybe other times). She frequented the place for over a year and became acquainted with lots of people; in other words, she became a familiar face.

Nearly a year and a half after I dragged her into this lounge, she married a man she had met there. As far as I know, she's still happily married to this day, and that's been more than 15 years now.

Many women have told me they don't like the shady characters they meet in bars. My advice here is to *change bars*. And as I stated before, you can meet shady characters at just about any singles (or marrieds) function you attend. So don't be misled or drop your guard just because of the party location. The SMART shady characters know they will take on an air of respectability when they attend church-sponsored events or other so-called "private" singles gatherings, masking their true character. And women at these types of events tend to let their guards down, and when they do . . . zingo! The shady guy moves in, and lord knows what can happen. I recommend that women be just as skeptical at church and private functions as they are in lounges—because lounges don't have a monopoly on "jerks."

Get to know the lounge owner, the bartenders, and the waitresses. Many times they can steer you away from the "creeps" and introduce you to the good guys.

On your first trip to a lounge, go with another woman—single or married doesn't matter—she's only there for moral support.

There's strength in numbers. But remember: A man will be much more hesitant about striking up a conversation with two women than he will with one. After you get to know and be known in the lounge that you have targeted, go alone and give the new "familiar faces" a chance to chat with you one-on-one. Also, go easy on the alcohol. It blurs your judgment. And if you are driving, go especially easy, or you may end up looking for Mr. Wonderful in the slammer.

✳ **Dear George:**

I agree with you that the best place to meet men nowadays is in a lounge. But where do we go? How do we go about it? How do we meet men? What do we say?

As far as how women do it or what they say to someone in a lounge depends, of course, on what type of women they are— whether they're the outgoing type or the shy, quiet type. But the first and most important thing for women to know is that they should sit— or stand—*at or near the bar*. If they hide themselves at a table in the far corner of the room, they're dead! Preferably, they should look for an empty seat at the bar, near someone of the opposite sex and in their approximate age group. And if there is only one seat next to him, ask him if the seat is taken. He'll probably respond that the seat is not taken, and this usually breaks the ice. He'll probably carry the conversation from there.

Here's a true scene I recently observed in a neighborhood lounge in a large city. I was sitting at this fairly deserted bar, when a lovely lady entered and sat about six stools away from me. Soon after, a man came in and sat around the bend in the bar, about two or three seats from her. After a few minutes had elapsed, the lady commented to him about the "handsome smile lines" he had in his face and asked him if he worked outdoors all his life? He told her what he did for a living and they started talking. By the time I left, about a half-hour later, they had become comfortable friends and had even made a date to go fishing together. I'm ashamed to say that I eavesdropped on their conversation. But I did so because she was so smooth at instantly winning a new friend. In fact, the man actually had a load of wrinkles on his face, but she turned them into "handsome smile lines." She said something *positive* and *pleasant*, and the conversation was off and running.

Some of you women are thinking, "Well, that's okay for the younger generation, who find it easier to talk to strangers. But how about those of us who are 30, 40, 50?" Well, the lady I referred to in this story was 73 years young, and the man with the smile lines was 67. Surprised? Don't be! It happens all the time.

If you want to strike up a conversation, do the following:

Don't start off by complaining about the weather, or the traffic, or things like that. He might have endured complaining clients all day long and doesn't need to listen to another complainer . . . especially during his free time.

Don't clunk down a huge saddlebag of a purse on the bar, taking up all the room. It makes it look like you are planning to camp out at the bar for the weekend. And don't put your purse on the empty seat next to you. It will defeat the possibility of a potential new acquaintance sitting next to you. If you don't have a small purse, then lock the "saddlebag" in the trunk of your car.

Don't let a stranger buy you a drink unless you REALLY want to spend more time chatting with him. If you accept his drink, chances are he's going to zero in on you and get his three bucks worth of conversation. And if he's a crashing bore, you're stuck . . . at least for as long as the drink holds out.

Don't be pushy. If a man doesn't appear to be interested in talking with you, then leave him alone. There'll be other days and other guys.

Speaking of "pushy," here's a story that happened to me. One day as I was driving down the street I suddenly got a number of brainstorms that I just HAD to get down on paper before I forgot them. A nearby lounge was the only place where I could write, so I went into the bar with my pad and pencil and began writing notes furiously, before I forgot all these wonderful ideas I had. I was obviously totally engrossed in what I was doing, when an obnoxious female came in and sat next to me. She unloaded her saddlebag all over the bar and demanded a drink from the bartender. Then (even though she noticed that I was writing like mad) she started to strike up a conversation with me. I tried to be polite and would nod or give her a quick comment to the string of complaints she was heaping on me about the weather, the traffic, and everything else under the sun, and then I'd return to my writing. Finally, she got the hint that I was busy and had to finish what I was doing. So she complained to the bartender that "some people don't have manners enough to talk with a lady," obviously referring to me.

I guarantee that this woman will NEVER meet a wonderful man who will become attracted to her, because she doesn't know how to be wonderful herself. She only cares about what she wants, to the exclusion of others.

✳ **Dear George:**

You always talk about meeting singles in lounges. What's wrong with meeting them at church activities? I think it's a better atmosphere.

I agree it's a better atmosphere. But you can't cuddle up with atmosphere on a cold winter night, because that's about all you'll find at most of the church functions I've attended . . . and I've been to a bunch!

It seems church groups don't attract the exciting, modern-day male or female because the church parties are usually so monastic, so puritanical—yes, even boring. They appear more as proselytizing endeavors than "parties." Singles go to a party for a *vacation*, not a *vocation*.

And, usually, church group singles events seem to border on immaturity. Some events include games that we played in grammar school, ice cream socials, box lunches (where the women end up sharing their lunches with each other because not enough men are attracted to the idea), hayrides with no hay, religious skits. I could go on and on. One church event featured "group" projects in which people were divided into separate groups to solve a Bible riddle or some similar "problem." I guess the idea was to get to know the opposite-sexers in your group a little better. But what happens if you have your eye on the gorgeous blonde in another group? You're stuck the whole evening in the group you got assigned to. By the time the evening is over, the blonde has lined up a date with someone in her group and leaves with him. It happens.

When a church group has a breakfast or dinner function, everyone enters and takes his or her seat at a table set for about fifty. So you only get to meet the people on either side of you—and maybe across the way. Church groups for the most part don't plan their events to appeal to your average single persons or their needs.

But I don't criticize without offering a solution. Following are some suggestions for how I think church-sponsored singles parties should be planned.

If it's going to be a sit-down meal, have it start out in a "cocktail party" type of atmosphere in which everyone mingles—on their feet—for about 45 minutes before they take their seats for the meal. Guests can walk around with a cup of coffee or a soda pop while they are mingling with the other guests in attendance.

Fill out a nametag for everyone as they enter. And put their business occupations under their names. It's a great conversation starter.

I like the idea of serving (or selling) beer and wine at these church parties because you'll attract more guests. And if you SELL these drinks at a profit, you'll help strengthen the club's treasury.

I remember once suggesting to a church group that they serve beer and wine at their singles parties. You'd have thought I was a heretic . . . or worse. Some said it would be a sin to serve alcoholic beverages at a Christian event. I couldn't help but remind them WHO changed water into wine at the marriage feast at Cana so that the wedding party could continue. Guess what answer I got to this one? Water wasn't changed into wine but only grape juice. They must be reading some Bible that's different from the one I was brought up on. Anyhow, except for the Episcopalians, Catholics, and Jews, it looks like serving beer and wine is a "no-no" at most other church functions.

The next thing these church party organizers have to decide is whether the party is going to be a prayer meeting or an honest to goodness singles party. If the object is to attract people to these parties and get them to come back and bring friends and grow larger, then they've got to go the singles party route. I have seen many, many singles turned off when they found that the singles party was more of a ruse to get these people into the sponsor's church and attend a church service. If I want to go to a prayer meeting or a church service, I've got plenty of churches around the corner I can attend much more conveniently. When I go to a singles party, I want it to be a "party." Besides, I think a church can accomplish more with a lot of "short blasts" of religion spread over many parties, rather than one big effort at one time, never to see the guests again.

Dancing is also important if you are going to get the guests coming back on a regular basis. I know of one church group that didn't allow dancing because they said it was immoral. So instead the singles got together for what they called a "bundling" party, where the couples wrapped themselves together in a blanket out on a moonlit lawn.

Now that's my idea of a great singles party! You avoid all the miscellaneous buildup and head straight for the sack.

To heck with dancing. From now on it's bundling for me. I wish I could remember what denomination that was.

✳ **Dear George:**

As a professional organist, I have played for many weddings. I always ask the bridal couple how they met. Many of them met in church-sponsored activities, at friends' homes, in college, at political meetings, at sports activities, even on blind dates. Frankly, I'd rather my daughters were introduced through mutual friends than by a bartender. Wake up girls! There is a world outside the dark bar scene.

Whoa! Hold it! I never said women SHOULD go to bars to meet more men. I only said it's the BEST PLACE to meet men. It would be nice if we all could meet our mates at the events you suggest, but let's be pragmatic. If we all waited to be invited to one of the functions you suggest, we'd never leave home; there just aren't enough of them geared to singles mingling.

Many church-sponsored singles parties have 50 women and 10 men in attendance, and they all seem to congregate in "hives." It's usually a very cold atmosphere, as though the sponsors didn't think we were even worth the bother to hang a piece of colored crepe paper to let us know this is a special party event.

And someone always manages to introduce the 70-year-old men to the 30-year-old women, and vice versa. You get the feeling that you must be the most hard up person in the world just for attending.

And how many cups of fruit punch or tea can one consume and still keep smiling? No one running these church parties seems to care or bother to take us singles seriously.

I've tried the Sunday morning coffee-after-church get-togethers, but they are basically for married couples. I feel like a hypocrite if I try to use these types of church socials for my own private life enhancement.

This letter writer wrote, "Wake up girls! There is a world outside the dark bar scene." I wish instead she had written, "Wake up *guys,* and support and attend all the quality singles activities that are sponsored not only by churches but also by other groups for the benefit of all singles." That's the biggest problem: Men don't attend these activities because no one makes a concentrated effort to attract them. And if the men don't attend, the women won't either . . . and the entire effort is doomed.

One last thing: You can't have the age disparities at these church functions like the ones I've seen so many times. You can't mix two or three generations and expect anything to happen. Music preferences are different. Tastes are different. Conversational subjects are different. If you organize church singles parties by age groups, you'll get lots more attention and interest.

We all need GOOD church-sponsored singles activities. I'll be the first one to shout it from the rooftops (I should say from the steeple tops). But the organizers have to realize that not everyone in attendance has aspirations of becoming a monk or a minister. Of the hundreds of church parties I have attended, it would appear that Reverend Moon and his followers have more fun at their functions than we do at the average church-sponsored singles function.

So until someone decides to run church activities more effectively and pay attention to the special needs of single people, one of the principal places to meet your Mr. or Ms. Wonderful, besides private singles parties or dances, is still in an upscale lounge I've been harping about.

And they really aren't all that dark!

* 7 *

Meeting Through Telephone Dating Services!

M AYBE I SHOULD CALL these "telephone/newspaper" dating services, since both media are involved. But whatever we call them, these are the ads that are run in a special section of the newspaper (often in the classified section) several days a week. These newspaper ads describe a potential date in some detail and provide a special "900" number that you can call to hear that person talking about him/herself in much more detail. If you like what you hear, you can then leave your own personal voice mail response along with your phone number.

The people who respond to these ads are charged anywhere from $2 to $5 per minute for their telephone time; the bill can mount very fast. In some newspapers, the person who placed the ad is also charged a per-minute fee to *retrieve* the phoned-in responses. If the ad is attractive and draws lots of attention, it can easily engender 30 or 40 responses which, when retrieving, can take as long as 60 to 80 minutes. Thus, the telephone bill can mount up much faster for the person who placed the ad, and this becomes somewhat of a deterrent to placing ads for anyone but the very well heeled. To alleviate this problem, more and more services are permitting the advertiser one free retrieval phone call per week. Some are placing a $5 or $10 limit on the amount an advertiser must pay each week to retrieve his or her messages. More and more are simply providing free, unlimited retrieval.

This relatively new method of meeting singles (it started in the early 1990s) quickly became a billion-dollar a year business and continues to grow for one simple reason: It's a good idea!

Telephone/newspaper ads have both benefits and drawbacks. One benefit is that when you call the person who placed the ad, you hear that person's voice mail describing him or herself and what he or she is looking for. If you don't like what you hear, you can hang up. It costs only a couple of dollars. And the person who placed the ad gets to hear the responders speak and describe themselves. A lot of what they say in their messages tells something about their character, their grammar, their education, and their attitude. The longer they talk, the more information you gather to decide whether or not you want to meet this person.

Another benefit is that everything is on a private basis, and you can usually arrange a date quickly and efficiently, with a minimum of muss and fuss.

One drawback for the responders is that they have to give their phone numbers to a stranger. This could be a problem, but since you get to hear the person talk, you can at least determine something about his/her character. If you have any doubts, you can always leave a work number or beeper number, although the latter may mark you as a suspicious, untrusting person and squelch the whole date right from the start.

A drawback for the advertiser is that he/she might have to listen to dozens of responses, which in addition to being costly can also be tiresome.

You readers know me well enough by now to know that I don't just listen to hearsay. I find things out for myself. So here's what I did. I placed ads in these "singles connections" in several newspapers to see what responses I'd get. I also responded to a lot of ads placed by women, and I researched what kinds of responses they got from their ads. Naturally, you are always going to get one or two "misfits" no matter what you do or where you go, but in all my research, I was surprised to find that 98 percent of all the people who placed or responded to these ads were top-quality, trustworthy, honest people. Honest!

My research covered over five hundred respondents, so I'm sure it's the largest (and only) survey of its kind. The women I talked to who had placed these ads also were surprised with the quality of the respondents, who were doctors, teachers, professional people, ministers—it was a real eye-opener. A few of the women I called were literally exhausted from handling the number of responses they received.

Here's an ad one woman placed:

> Divorced, white female, age 42, but looks and feels like 32. Tall, thin, cute, vivacious. Seeks tall, witty, intelligent, attractive man for fun and possible soulmate. Are you out there?

She received 60 calls the first week and became totally frustrated because she knew she couldn't see them all. So she judged by the message they left on her voice mail who were the best ones to call back. She spoke to 30 of the men and made a date for coffee or cocktails with five of the 30. Of the five "finalists," she continued to date two of them for many months.

Another woman ran this ad:

> Divorced lady, 40-something, seeks tall, handsome, intelligent man for dating, and for life.

She received 28 calls the first two weeks but wasn't as lucky. She felt that most respondents sounded weird, and she met only three of the men for drinks/coffee. One man, a retired colonel, had a drinking problem; whenever he got drunk, he'd call her box number, which cost her money when she retrieved her messages. Finally, she returned his call and told him to call her at work (where she could then refuse his calls without wasting any more money on her retrieval services). It worked and he stopped calling her ad.

Another woman ran this ad:

> **Shy but wild! Attractive, talented, witty, wealthy, single white female looking for a male interested in boating, biking, and art. Interested in conversation with possibility of a transformational relationship.**

She was overwhelmed with 62 calls the first week. Most wanted to find out what transformational meant. Though it doesn't mean anything special, it certainly piqued the interest of an awful lot of men. She personally met 10 of the respondents and dated several of them regularly. She felt she got more than her money's worth from this ad.

These few examples should give you an idea of what kind of ads pulled the biggest responses. But keep in mind that although 98 percent of the respondents were top quality and aboveboard, some of the women I talked to had a few weird people call their ads, and you may too. One 30-year-old woman returned a call to a respondent who *sounded* as though he also was about 30 years old, and she made a date to meet him at a restaurant. It turned out that he was 80 years old and married and that he wanted "something on the side." He started to fondle her, so she slapped his face and walked out on him. (EDITOR'S NOTE: Must be that damned VIAGRA again.)

Another woman received a call from a married man (42 years old), and she unwittingly responded. He complained that his wife had gotten fat and let herself go and that as a result, he had no sex life in his marriage. She told him as far as she was concerned, he wasn't going to have any OUTSIDE his marriage either and hung up on him.

One caller (age 44) said the world was inhabited by robots and that people had been taken away on spaceships. (She hung up too.)

Another woman returned a call to a professional man in his 40s who—after talking to him for 20 minutes—asked her how long they'd have to wait before getting married. He could tell just by talking to her that she was the one for him. (Hang up again.)

The nice thing about placing these ads is that you don't *have* to respond to all the callers and you don't *have* to give your full name or phone number when you do . . . until you know it's okay to do so.

Now let's look at the results I had when I ran my own ads in these same newspaper sections, looking for my Ms. Wonderful. But, first of all, let me assure you that my research was not a subterfuge that wasted the respondent's time and money. First of all, I really was interested in meeting a lady for a one-on-one relationship, so my ad was honest. And for those who responded and met my specifications, I took them all out for a drink (or two or three) and gave them a free copy of my first edition of *Single Again*. So if they spent $2 or $3 responding to my ad, they received in return the equivalent of $4 to $15. I felt that was fair. Anyway, here's the ad I ran several times in several different newspapers:

> **READY TO SETTLE DOWN**
> Successful, white male executive, 56, 6 ft., 195 lbs., has been single for 13 years now and ready for a one-on-one relationship with a SLIM lady age 42–52. I'm a giving person, great cuddler w/good sense of humor. If you are the same, let's get together for a drink.

My voice mail message expanded on these points from my printed ad. I asked the caller to please give me her age, height, and weight when she responded, along with her home telephone number.

I have to tell you that I was overwhelmed with responses to these ads. More than 157 women called and left messages on my voice mail. Several were so nervous they forgot to leave their home phone numbers, and I couldn't reach them. But 157 did! Five respondents called from states as far as one thousand five hundred miles away. While I sympathized with the long-distance phone bills they must have run up, I felt it was unnecessary to return their calls, since I had so many local callers.

I called all who satisfied my requirements—a mind-numbing total of 83 women—and met them for a drink at a mutually convenient place (six of them stood me up! Oh well!).

While I advertised for women age 42 to 52, a total of 27 women were older than 52, and 9 were under 42. I purposely advertised for a SLIM lady—even capitalizing it in my ad—and received 70 phone calls from women who were not even close to being slim. Four of the respondents refused to give their height and weight, which automatically made me suspicious.

Here are a few more of the "interesting" comments left on my voice mail from some of the respondents: One said my ad sounded arrogant (why in the world did she waste a toll call to bawl me out???). One said height and weight were superficial and wouldn't tell me either (she must have had something to hide, I figured). One bawled me out for suggesting that we get together for a "drink" (she said drinking was the cause of her three marriage break-ups, or did she DRIVE them to drink!). One was a 27-year-old in drug rehab, looking for a sugar daddy. Several said they were unhappy to be making this call. One lady said she spent $22 on her call because she kept changing and erasing her message in an attempt to get it to sound right. A few women bawled me out for stating that I was successful, saying such information would attract gold diggers.

For the life of me, I can't understand why these unpleasant women would spend their money on a toll call to bitch at someone they had never even met! They must have known that I would never return their call to make a date. Strange, isn't it? But, luckily, they were in the minority.

My advice, after fielding 157 calls, is to be pleasant, happy, and optimistic that this is the last such call you will ever have to make, because your "Mr. or Ms. Wonderful" is on the other end of the line.

The average female caller to my ads was married 1.7 times. Two had been married five times, and one had never been married. And, as I said before, 98 percent of them were fine, high-quality people I'd be proud to bring home to mother. I arranged to meet each caller at a restaurant or lounge for a drink. I disdained having dinner or a meal with any of them, since they all were blind dates, so to speak, and both of us might not want to spend that amount of time together. Also, I had too many respondents to be able to spend that much time. In fact, I suggested to each "date" that we only spend 15 minutes on our initial get-together so that the "clock"—not one of us—would decide when the date was over. This way, if we saw that the person wasn't for us, no one would hurt the other's feelings by cutting the date short. We let the clock do it so that we both could bow out gracefully, saving a lot of bruised egos and hard feelings. Also, with the large numbers of women I had to meet, this seemed the most equitable way to do it.

I ended up meeting dozens of really wonderful women with whom I have enjoyed some very memorable times. Whether any of them is my Ms. Wonderful remains to be seen.

It cost me over $400 to respond to all the calls, but when you consider all the wonderful new friends I made as a result, it's really quite a bargain.

Speaking as an experienced bachelor who has researched every possible method of meeting single women, it appears that telephone/newspaper dating services are the next best way to go after singles parties and upscale lounges. And it's a heck of a lot more convenient.

✳ 8 ✳

Meeting Through Magazine and Newspaper Ads

LONELY HEARTS ADS, or "mail-order" dating ads, as I call them, are a big business in this country. But I personally feel that these types of ads are soon going to be replaced by the newspaper/telephone ads described in Chapter 7, at least in the *local* newspaper classified sections.

However, a large number of singles still prefer placing or answering these lonely hearts ads, so let's take a look at them.

Mail-order dating ads run every day in the classified sections of the newspaper; you mail your response to a blind box number in care of the newspaper. If one is going to try these ads, I think it is more feasible and more economical to run them in the *local* newspapers, as opposed to national singles publications. I know of one woman who ran such an ad in a national singles magazine. She received several dozen replies, all asking for a photograph. The only good photo she had was one taken 20 years earlier when, she was pretty, slim, and trim, so she sent it out. One man, who was seeking a slim mate, bit. He flew into town to meet his unseen Ms. Wonderful. Imagine his chagrin when he stepped off the airplane to be greeted by an overweight woman who bore little resemblance to her photo.

If he had answered only LOCAL ads, he could have saved the long-distance airfare and the problem of rattling around alone in a strange city—after terminating his date.

The biggest complaint I hear—from men and women—is that the photographs they get are either old or retouched, and bear no similarity to the person in person. Here's one way to steer clear of outdated photos. Ask respondents to have the photo taken while they hold up the front page of *today's* newspaper. This way, you can check the headlines to see whether the photograph is current.

Several years ago, I tested a classified dating ad to see what results I would get, and they were predictable. Here is the ad I ran:

> Financially secure, attractive professional in 50s, is tired of the singles scene and interested in a long-range commitment with the right person. Loves parties, golf, tennis, bridge, dancing, travel. Interested in pretty, warm woman in her 40s who shares my interests. Send recent photo and phone number for prompt reply. Tell me something about yourself.

While I do really enjoy the things I listed, I purposely wrote this ad to get the greatest number of replies from the widest array of women.

I received 26 replies, but only 12 bothered to enclose photos. I wrote to the 14 who neglected to send photos, but none of them would agree to send me one. In fact, two of them replied they had already done enough just by answering my ad and weren't about to send me a photograph. It sounded like they wanted to start our relationship off on an argumentative basis, so I quickly rejected them as being negative women and concentrated on the rest.

Ninety percent of the respondents gave their first names only. Two gave their addresses, but all gave their phone numbers, possibly thinking this was the safe way to respond to someone they hadn't met. What most didn't realize was that I could go to the public library and, using the cross-reference directory, learn their full names and addresses via their phone numbers. In fact, I went to the library to prove it and found everyone's name and home address in about 10 minutes. The gals who thought they were protecting themselves by not giving full names and addresses blew it by giving their home phone numbers.

For security reasons, it is much better for women to give only their office number and extension, or a post office box number. Then, when they hear from the advertiser, they can get *his* phone number and call him back.

Though I advertised for a woman in her 40s, most of the replies were from women over 50, with a few over 60.

One lady gave her bra and cup size. Even though they sounded enormous, I didn't respond.

I called one woman who looked and sounded good (she was 39), but her parents answered the telephone and grilled me so unmercifully that I never did get a chance to talk to the respondent. Not wanting to start off a relationship with a built-in "in-law" problem, I never called her back.

I selected six women to go out with. I didn't call anyone who didn't send a photo, figuring they had something to hide. Of the six I took out, only one shared any of the hobbies or interests I had mentioned in the ad. All the rest were just covering the market, hoping they would hit on something.

One of the women continued to call me at least once a week, asking when I was going to take her out again. Another admitted that the photo she had sent was over 15 years old (it no longer looked anything like her). Another who wrote a very humorous letter turned out to be the biggest grouch. The one lady who shared my interests was also the most pleasant, and we've had some good times together on occasional dates over the years.

❈ Dear George:

I had several sour experiences answering "mate wanted" ads in newspapers. The girls seem to make themselves appear better than they really are. One lady I met was on her way to get her stomach stapled so that she could solve her huge weight problem. Another just wanted a man—any man. She would have taken me if I was Jack the Ripper. Another was sorry that she had run the ad. It was such a waste of time. Tell your readers to try the bar scene. It's more reliable, and at least you can see what you're getting.

I've put together the five commandments for answering a mail-order dating ad. Judging from the many comments I get, I think these commandments apply to just about all situations:

1. If a photograph is requested, by all means, send one. A full-length photo is best. If you don't look good enough to send a photo, then do something about your appearance first and then take the photo. Any snapshot is acceptable. It doesn't have to be a fancy studio shot.
2. Give your facts and statistics briefly and pleasantly.
3. If you don't want the person to know your full name and address, then list your work phone number and extension, or give a post office box number.
4. Pay attention to the hobbies and interests listed in the ad. Surely you can find *something* similar in your backgrounds that you can emphasize in your letter of reply.
5. If you are older or younger than the age range stipulated, then acknowledge the age difference. Then explain in your letter that, for example, you LOOK or ACT the age he/she requested. Such explanations will give you a better chance to sell yourself.

✳ Dear George:

I placed an ad with a group of sorority sisters in a lonely-hearts column. We got a mailbag full of responses. I pulled out one letter and said, "This one is mine." It turned out I was right. The man who wrote the letter and I were engaged for 3 years. The ad continued to get responses for 2 more years.

Never mind your love life. I'd like to meet the person who wrote your ad and hire her to write copy for me.

One female reader of my newspaper column offered to run an ad in her local newspaper to find out what a woman might expect from a lonely-hearts ad. She was 56 years young, very attractive and upbeat, and very intelligent . . . able to converse with anyone about any subject. She was a very positive person, always pleasant and smiling.

Her ad stated that she was above average in intelligence, financially and emotionally secure, and looking for a man with the same traits. She disdained the "foxy lady" approach, even though she could have qualified here too.

She received 22 replies and met with 19 of the respondents (she couldn't locate the other three). She met each of them over coffee, breakfast, or lunch in a public restaurant, and she always drove herself. Nine of the men she rejected right away as being incompatible.

The men ranged in age from 48 to 73; the average was 59 years. She talked to each man on the telephone at great length before she met him, and this gave her pretty good insight into what kind of person he'd be and whether she would meet him for a meal or just a cup of coffee. She didn't want to spend too much of her time with the ones who didn't initially sound like they were her kind of man.

The list of men reads like a "who's who" of dates. They included a retired college president, a radio station owner, several corporate owners and developers, school teachers, a pilot, a male model, and computer experts, and they all loved traveling and all the other interests she mentioned in her ad. She really hit the jackpot.

Four of the men ended up proposing marriage, and she dated three of them for a long time. When critiquing the respondents, she said that all were sincere and looking for a lasting relationship rather than a one-night stand. Many wanted to know how they compared to the competition, showing, she said, that men have many of the same feelings of inadequacy as women and were willing to admit it. None were bar hoppers, but all thought it was perfectly respectable to answer a dating ad.

A few, however, became openly hostile when discussing ex-wives, which seemed to put her on the spot. Her word of advice here was to tell men not to discuss their ex-wives on a date. It's boring and in bad taste, especially since the "ex" isn't around to defend herself.

This story ended up in a strange twist of fate. (Remember! Everything in this book is a true story.) This classy lady, who had so many great respondents to her newspaper ad wanting to marry her, eventually met a widower on his first visit to a singles happy hour—*in a lounge, of all places*—and married him 5 months later. They spent their honeymoon on his 50-foot yacht.

Who says the bar scene doesn't work?

✳ **Dear George:**

I'm a 36-year-old male, 6 ft. 2 in., and considered good looking. I'm interested in finding a lady in the 25 to 35 age range. I have taken out two dating ads. I got three responses on one and four on the other, and none panned out. I also answered several ads and got next to no response. I work with my hands and only earn $18,000 a year, so I'm low on the totem pole. It seems that women have their pick of men and won't talk to anyone making less than $50,000.

This is America where you can always improve your job status with a little extra effort or education. Next time you answer an ad, don't mention your job status or salary or type of work. If you are of good character (and you sound like you are), that will end up being more important than your job. You can always change your job, but you can't change your personality. I know plenty of people who make mucho bucks but who aren't worth two cents as human beings.

Try this in a few ads you reply to and see what happens. Send your photograph (neatly dressed) and mention only your age, hobbies, interests, church affiliation, name, and address. It should work!

Here's a story about mail-order dating ads that will really slay you. It's a true story; I personally verified all the facts. (Everything in this book is true, remember?)

Jim (not his real name) was a wealthy middle-aged rancher in a medium-sized Midwestern town. Despite his wealth and his expensive lifestyle, he had trouble meeting women and—once he did—keeping them interested in him. He was fairly self-centered (as many millionaires are), and women found this to be a turnoff. In fact, they found it boring. With all his wealth and all the creature comforts he could offer, after nearly 10 years of searching, he was unable to find someone who would go out with him more than three or four times.

> Dying millionaire in 50s, 6ft tall. Seeks a trim, attractive lady under 50 to save him from death by boredom. Send photo and details to . . .

He was becoming frantic! One day, he got a "brainstorm" and wrote the following lonely hearts ad:

He placed this ad in the classified section of a national daily newspaper and received a phenomenal response. Exactly 121 women answered his ad, perhaps hoping to cash in on the largess of this "dying" millionaire. (He, of course, wasn't really ill, just dying for female companionship.) Following are some of the responses:

One woman wrote from a penitentiary, asking him for money to buy a new RV after she was paroled. She enclosed several intimate photographs that must have been taken by her gynecologist.

Another cute respondent sent him a photograph—complete with pasties in all the right places. And every month she followed up with a new photo of herself, with more pasties in the right places. Even though he never met her personally, she must have spent a hundred bucks on her photo-of-the-month campaign.

Many of the respondents were convicts, mostly people in jail for writing bad checks. A number of women wrote to bawl him out for appealing to "fortune hunters."

A husband and wife team invited him to join them in a ménage à trois. It sounded pretty sick.

A secretary wanted $4,500 for breast augmentation surgery and ended her letter saying that she would be happy to meet him in person after the operation to say "thanks for the mammaries."

Several women wanted to be "kept" and gave very graphic descriptions of their "abilities."

He received a number of letters from women in foreign countries. The farthest was from China, where a Beijing University graduate offered to be his "lady."

Many described hardships or economic problems they or their families faced and offered just about everything in exchange for a little monetary assistance.

The sad thing about this story is that some of these desperate women seemed not to understand that the man was being playful, perhaps a bit devious. It was like offering a bone to a puppy dog and pulling it away just as he goes for it.

The world of mail-order dating can be a strange world, populated by some strange people.

At the top of this chapter, I stated that I wasn't a big fan of mail-order dating ads. You might be surprised that I have these feelings after reading a few of the success stories, which show that these ads can really draw attention . . . and results.

My feelings about this type of singles activity stems from an experience I once had in a lounge. A woman joined two men sitting next to me and pulled out a large envelope stuffed with replies to a dating ad she had run in a local newspaper. She and the two men proceeded to open and read aloud the dozen or so letters she received, to the amusement of everyone else around the bar. They made fun of the respondents, even to the point of mentioning their names. What was meant to be a private letter by the writer was being shared with everyone at the bar.

But, in fact, when you answer a dating ad, you never know the type of person who placed it.

9

Meeting Through Singles Clubs and Organizations

IN EVERY CITY, TOWN, AND HAMLET there probably exists a so-called "singles club," where supposedly lonely singles can gather and socialize with other singles with the same tastes and of the same age group for nominal annual dues. Do they succeed? Read on, McDuff.

Dear George:

I'm tired of the bar scene. My church doesn't have a singles group, and I can't afford dating services. I have heard about singles clubs. What do you think of them?

I don't think much of *most* singles clubs. I have found that for the most part they are run by domineering people with strong maternal instincts who like to boss their flocks around and take charge of other people's lives. Their demeanor usually chases away the *good* males and females, and all that are left are those who can't make it anywhere else.

Quite often the club members act as if they are privileged people who are superior to "nonclub" people. Most of them drive me nuts. However, like with everything else, I have to qualify my remarks. If the singles club is formed for a good reason or provides an extra service that the members couldn't get otherwise, then I think they're great. Ski clubs, bicycle clubs, scuba diving clubs, travel clubs, and other specialized clubs afford the members special activities or group discounts that make membership a good deal. Plus, the members get to meet and associate with other people of similar interests. I agree with and wholeheartedly endorse membership in these types of singles clubs. In fact, I love 'em!

Clubs that benefit charities and worthy causes are also good; they form a pool of volunteers who are ready and willing to help out in various fundraising endeavors. I also heartily endorse these kind of clubs. If there is one in your town, join it!

It's the *social* singles clubs that leave me cold. Although I do know of several of them around the country that are well organized and run with the members' best interests at heart, the vast majority of those I've heard of or have attended have actually been *detrimental* to the members' well-being. I realize the importance most women place in dancing—men too—and a lot of these social clubs provide this outlet for their members. That's okay, too, if it stops there. But I've seen many instances in which even these club dances and "socials" became so inbred after awhile that all the members know in advance who to expect to be in attendance at each affair, and they tend to shun any newcomers of their own sex, for fear of competition.

In this regard, belonging to the singles club becomes stifling and actually *inhibits* the members' chances of getting out and meeting new people. The singles club member becomes a prisoner of his/her own club.

✳ Dear George:

As a woman, all the singles club parties I've been to have about 10 women to every man. Are there singles MEN'S clubs around that I don't know about? Where do all the men go?

They obviously don't go where you go. And if there's a singles club for men, I don't want to know about it.

It's an age-old problem that just keeps getting worse . . . the lop-sided ratio of single women to single men in the world. This problem carries over to the vast majority of singles clubs; there are far too many women enrolled and far too few men. It sometimes can be embarrassing, especially for men in senior citizen clubs, where they are swamped with women the moment they enter the party, each woman looking for a dancing partner. As I said before, "social" singles clubs leave a lot to be desired, for both sexes.

✳ **Dear George:**

I'm happily married, but I read your column always with plea-sure. l wish I had the kind of help you give way back in 1980, when I was trying any way possible to meet new friends. My suggestion for people wanting to meet new people is to join an organization or become a volunteer in places where they will meet all kinds of new people. I used to go to the park and donate my time working (mostly with men). You can also meet some nice people giving your time to the Red Cross, Salvation Army, etc.

Good idea. It's like having your own private singles club that only YOU know about.

✳ **Dear George:**

I'm not aware of any singles clubs in my area. It occurs to me there is a need for such a club. Occasionally, l think I'd like to start one with the help of friends. Can you tell me some of the necessary procedures for starting one? Is an age group important, or is it best to mix all ages? What kinds of meetings are most popular? Where does one begin?

I'm familiar with your city and happen to know several singles groups that are affiliated with churches and civic groups. I also know that at a party cosponsored by two of these groups, the ratio in atten-dance was 75 women to 6 men. As I've stated, therein lies the problem of starting or maintaining a singles club—that is, getting more good men to attend.

If you can figure out a way to get good men to come—and come back—you'll get the attractive women to return, and you'll have a most successful club.

But to pull it off, you're going to have to do a lot of "planning in keeping with a *man's* point of view" (sorry about that!). I have often heard women complain about men watching Sunday football on television or about their involvement in some outdoor activity not necessarily to a woman's liking. Well, why not face reality and schedule some outdoor activities or Sunday afternoon football parties as part of your social activities? You'll at least get the men's attention. Serving some food at halftime will keep them there, too. And not allowing pushy or complaining women at your parties will help bring the men back.

I can hear some of you ladies saying, "Who in the hell do you men think you are that we women have to plan our parties to fit in with your male egos and idiosyncrasies? Who's paying attention to OURS?" Well, earlier in this book I said I would tell things they way they ARE, not necessarily the way we'd LIKE them to be in a perfect world. When a woman is *dating* a man, he should pay attention to *her* wants and desires. But we're talking about singles clubs in this chapter, not dating. And, in fact, if you want to attract the widest number of desirable males to your club functions, YOU HAVE TO PLAN THEM TO BE ATTRACTIVE TO A MAN'S POINT OF VIEW!

It seems so logical, yet I have been to scores of singles club parties in which the women in charge were determined NOT to give in to "male favoritism" and simply did their own thing, the same as if they were sponsoring a ladies luncheon or some similar female event. I can honestly report that I don't know of one of these social singles clubs that is still in existence at this writing. They all died on the vine from lack of interest; the men weren't interested in attending the events, and the women got bored seeing the same women over and over. Like it or not, if you are going to have a truly "social" singles club, you need both sexes equally represented in attendance.

Now let's get back to looking at other ways to get—and keep— a balance that will keep your social club growing and healthy.

Another way to attract good men is to hold Dutch treat "happy hour" from 5:00 P.M. to 7:00 P.M. on a weekday at a centrally located member's home or at a bar or lounge. Men will more readily stop on their way home from work than go to some late-night activity during the week. So will women.

If you can get a celebrity, sports star, or someone with some notoriety to attend your parties, so much the better. It will add stature to your events and make them more appealing. Be sure to mention them every chance you get in your announcements and mailings.

Age is important, but it's also a ticklish subject. If you are going to shoot for the "over 55" age group, be aware that there are many more women in this group than men (because you gals outlive us guys). And in many cases, the female members tend to develop negative attitudes because there are so few men around.

If you are aiming for the "under 30" or the "30 to 40" age group, be sure that most of the people at your parties are REALLY in this age group and that the music and all the activities are geared toward them; otherwise, they'll leave you in the dust. I've seen it happen many times. A 30-year-old will walk into a party, planned supposedly for his or her age group, look around for about 10 seconds to check out the age group and the type of music being played, and then walk out. Unless the room is jam-packed with people of the aimed-for age group, you will not find support for your get-together. It seems like a vicious circle.

My suggestion to this writer was to aim her efforts at the 40 to 55 age group. They seem to be the most supportive and most active, as well as the most flexible, positive thinkers. However, those over 55 should not be excluded. Just be sure they know that they have to be able to follow the direction your club is heading. Several times I've seen oldsters at a gathering of younger singles *demand* that the band play music from the 1940s. Some people tend to think only of themselves instead of the majority, and that's a shame. This kind of person will kill any singles club, so it's best to exclude them from the start.

It all boils down to determining what age group will support your activities best and then not wavering in your efforts to attract them.

Now the next question: What kinds of get-togethers are the most popular? That depends on the group's goals. If you are aiming at the younger folks, beach parties or parties in the park with some other sports activity on the agenda work very well. House parties and Friday happy hours (starting at 5:00 P.M.) work well with all age groups. Dances are great, too, but they are expensive to put on.

For some strange reason, dances and parties on Friday nights outdraw those on Saturday nights by three or four to one. The explanation I've heard most for this is that Saturday is usually considered "date night." Even if singles don't have a date, many won't admit it publicly, and their egos keep them home alone; they'd rather skip the party than let everyone know they don't have a date. Strange, isn't it?

To keep your parties out of a rut and from becoming repetitious ho-hum affairs, always offer something fresh, new, and exciting. And it's most important to have several pleasant, attractive greeters at all the functions. Be sure they personally greet everyone, female AND male, as they enter. And write out a name tag for every guest, listing the type of business he/she is in on the tag. It's a great conversation starter among strangers at a party.

I have attended many singles parties where I didn't know anybody, and nobody made any effort to make me feel welcome or to introduce me to someone. Usually, in such cases, a new guest will walk around the room several times, sample a few hors d'oeuvres, and leave, never to be seen again. Welcoming is most important.

Where do you begin to start a singles club? If it were up to me, I'd contact a popular local upscale lounge (here I go again) and ask to be allowed free use of a private area of the establishment for a singles happy hour with cash bar. (The reason I would use a bar or lounge is because they have all the facilities to serve a wide variety of all types of refreshments, and possibly hors d'oeuvres, saving the club organizer from having to stock up on a large variety of refreshments at a big cash outlay to the fledgling club. Also, there is better parking, more atmosphere, and better recognition by most potential members.) I'd ask the bar owner to include a mention of your singles party in his or her newspaper ads. In addition, I'd run a classified ad in the personal section of the local newspapers announcing this charter meeting of your singles group. I'd try to have some dance music if possible, and I'd do some of the things I mentioned previously. I would also get the name, address, and phone number of everyone who shows up. Thus, you have a mailing list from which to work, and you're off and running.

You noticed, I'm sure, that I previously criticized the basic idea of social singles clubs in general and that I also said that I don't criticize without offering a constructive solution. So here it is. I recommend that *all* singles clubs in the United States and Canada, unless you are a sports or travel club, adhere to the following recommendation, regardless of the age group of locale: Align your group with a good cause and become one or their fund-raising arms, for example, singles against cancer, singles for cerebral palsy research, or singles against Alzheimer's disease. There are hundreds of good causes that you can hook up with. Be sure that you pick a charity that is easily recognizable in your area (e.g., a singles group in Georgia organized to help fight Alaskan hoof and mouth disease is doomed to failure).

Then, when you decide which charity you want to work with, ask the director of that charity's local office to become "executive director" of your singles group. Most will readily agree to work with you, since their basic job is raising funds and dispensing them, and your group is there to help raise funds for them.

Instead of your group having a president and a slate of officers— who often try to *run* everything and everyone—set up a board of committees, with a different board member handling membership, or dues, or party scheduling, or outside fund-raising events, and so on, working in close conjunction with and under the supervision of the executive director of the charity.

But here is where you can score the most for your charity and for your singles members. Now that you are affiliated with a good cause, you can usually get contributions of time, space, products, and publicity from local businesses, local media, and local business leaders (many of whom are single and would probably make good members). You can probably get a local advertising agency to donate time to help your club put on dynamite dances, parties, and fund-raisers. Now, instead of running a small, uninspiring singles club, you can be running a worthwhile organization with plenty of prestige, attracting many more top-quality men and women. It's my guess that men will attend a fund-raiser or a charitable event 10 times faster than they will an ordinary singles dance or party. If for no other reason, it saves their macho egos. Many men don't think they NEED to go to a singles club event, but going to a singles *charity* event is a different, if you will, ball game. It makes them feel generous and civic minded. Many single women feel that way too.

But a word of caution: Don't make the fund-raiser sound like it's going to cost the attendee an arm and a leg. Charge the normal fee that you would charge for any singles dance and give the proceeds to your charity. Chances are that you'll have much larger crowds than normal and will be able to raise more for your cause. And while I keep harping on the need for men to attend these singles activities, like it or not, women need men for dancing partners, especially for the slow dances.

✳ **10** ✳
Meeting Through Professional Dating Services

ONE OF MY SINGLES COLUMN READERS gave me some information about the *real* costs of joining a popular nationally recognized singles dating service. The one he told me about advertises their service quite extensively on television and is probably one of the better-known services around the country. They advertise a "come-on" price in their ads, but I don't think you can rely on these prices.

They'll usually have two or more packages to sell. Of the two they'll usually discuss, one guarantees that you'll meet at least 3 people a month (36 a year), for a yearly enrollment fee of nearly a thousand dollars. This comes out to about $30 per introduction.

The other package guarantees that you'll meet at least one new person a month for 9 months, (hmmm, I wonder why 9 months?), giving you a total of nine new acquaintances for a fee of a little over $400. This comes to nearly $50 per introduction.

And, of course, there's always a "catch." The catch here is that the dates you are introduced to may live as far away as 50 miles. That's a heck of a long trip for a blind date, as far as I'm concerned.

I've got a great idea! Instead of spending this $400 for nine blind dates, I think it would be better if you took 80 five-dollar bills (totaling $400), wrote your name and phone number in the margin of each bill, and stood on a street corner and passed them out to everyone who looked pretty or handsome. At least you would know that anyone who bites is at least an attractive date and that they're from your locale. I think you might actually get quite a few people responding. Anyway, it's just an idea.

Usually, more women than men enroll in these matchmaking services, and they usually have a devil of a time trying to find enough men to go around. Thus, these services usually offer the men a huge discount to join, because they know the men will be worked to death with all the women they are going to be introduced to.

Dating services are sort of like employment agencies. If they send you around to enough potential employers (or potential dates in this case), one of them might stick. But the odds are that after you've spent a year with a dating service, you will have been rejected so many times by so many prospective dates that your self-esteem may become shattered.

I remember receiving a questionnaire from a "highly respected" dating service. It had about fifty questions relating to my background, needs, and desires. My answers were to be fed into a computer and *voila*, the printout would list my perfect mate, including her name, address, and phone number.

I contacted a lady friend of mine who had also received the same questionnaire in the mail. We each agreed to fill in identical answers for all the questions. Surely the computer would quickly match us up. Even a child of 10, when comparing our answers—our likes and dislikes, our wants and desires—would immediately surmise that we were truly made for each other . . . a match made in heaven.

Not so! This dating service had other plans for me. They wanted to spread this male around to keep as many women happy as possible . . . and keep them enrolled in the service. Then, perhaps, after I had burned myself out squiring all their conscripts, they would find my perfect match, my lady friend with the identical questionnaire, and we'd live happily ever after (and we'd be expected to state this in their testimonial ads, you can be sure).

I think you can save all the money you'd spend on these dating services if you follow the tips in this book. (And feel free to mail me a check for the amount of money you saved!)

* 11 *

Meeting on Cruises, in Supermarkets, and in Nudist Camps

THESE THREE ARE PROBABLY the least likely places for you to meet your Mr. or Ms. Wonderful, for a number of reasons. Cruises are great, but their prices are often out of reach of the mainstream single person. Supermarkets—unless they have a specified singles night—are places that most single men go in and out of as quickly as possible, so there isn't much time to socialize. And nudist camps? . . . well!

Meeting on Singles Cruises

* Dear George:

Are ocean cruises a good place to meet women? I've heard pro and con.

It's very easy to meet women on a cruise ship on the high seas, mainly because they don't have anywhere else to go once the ship leaves port. The one drawback is that when the cruise is over, the woman returns to her hometown, which is usually located in another state, so you don't accomplish much in the long run.

However, in spite of this, I thoroughly recommend singles cruises, or just cruises in general, since there are usually plenty of single people aboard ship. Read on.

If it's your first cruise and you're not accustomed to attending singles parties or dances, I'd suggest you get your feet wet by attending some sort of singles get-together before you go. This way, you'll learn how things go and how singles react to each other. It will help you feel more comfortable on the cruise, since you'll better know how to act or react, and you'll get off to a good start, without wasting valuable time.

I think the "windjammer" cruises are the best as far as getting to know everyone on board ship. The age ranges are usually in the under 50 group, and it is suggested that you have good "sea legs" since the ships are replicas of old sailing ships and have a tendency to rock and roll on the high seas. Also, the sleeping accommodations are rather cramped, which can be good or bad, depending on whom you are cramped with. It's more of a working cruise than a luxury cruise, but if your Mr/Ms. Wonderful is on board, you'll sure know it in a hurry.

I have run 27 singles ocean cruises, and my favorites are the gigantic luxury liner cruises to the Bahamas, Mexico, Bermuda, Hawaii, Caribbean, and so on. They have plenty of dancing, sun-bathing, and activities. And every cruise ship has a singles party the first evening out of port so that all singles aboard can meet each other (or at least look over each other). It gets the cruise off on the right foot.

The main reason I prefer large cruise ships over the smaller vessels is that they are more stable in the water and don't rock and sway as much. It's not worth being on a cruise if all the single women are laid up in their staterooms seasick and all the single men are barfing over the rail.

The minimum cruise time should be 3 days. Any cruise less than that doesn't give you enough time to survey the situation and set your sights on some lovely young thing (or handsome hunk, for you gals).

And don't forget! Single women on a cruise are just as interested in meeting men as we men are in meeting them. So there is less pretense on a cruise. Let's face it. No single person takes a cruise just to stare at the ocean.

I've seen a number of great relationships—even marriages—result from singles cruises. And those who didn't end up in a serious relationship nevertheless had a great time during the cruises. I recommend cruises for singles of all ages.

Let me mention one type of cruise that is becoming very popular lately. I'll call it the "happy widow" cruise. These cruises recruit widows and other single women as passengers and guarantee them a certain number of dances each evening with a number of different male partners in their age range. Naturally, the women pay a premium price for this "dance/dating" service and, judging from the number of women who take these cruises, they don't seem to mind it.

The men who are recruited to be their dancing partners get to go on the cruises gratis, and, in addition, are given from $25 to $100 a day for pocket money. The men's only obligation is to dance with a certain number of women each evening, usually 6 to 10 women. Then, when the men have fulfilled their obligation, they can spend the rest of the night (in addition to the days) mingling with the rest of the passengers on board. A few cruise lines require these escorts to accompany the ladies in the daytime as well, or even to show them the sights on shore at various ports.

The cruise directors and travel agents who put these cruises together usually screen the men quite thoroughly to be sure they know how to dance, know their manners, and don't mind dancing with all types and sizes of women—at least once.

This might seem like it's a good deal for the men. But after hearing tales about some of the verbal abuse that is heaped on them by some of these "happy" widows, they are forced to dance with, I don't think I'd like the job, at least not until they also screen the "happy" widows.

Meeting in Supermarkets

✳ **Dear George:**

I was shopping in a supermarket, when another shopper asked me if I was single. I said I was, and he asked me to dinner. I was so shocked that I told him I was already taken, even though I'm not. What should I have done?

I think you should either change supermarkets or let the rest of the single women know where you shop.

I've heard that shopping is the coming fad in singles mingling, but I can't prove it, and I don't really have any research that shows that it is a good place to meet singles. I remember once while I was shopping in the produce department of a local supermarket, a lady came up to me and asked whether MacIntoshes are good for cooking. She obviously was trying to strike up a conversation among "us singles," like she'd heard so much about. But I guess I blew it! I told her that if you cook a MacIntosh, you might melt the keyboard and ruin the microchips. She thought I was nuts! I guess some single shoppers don't have a sense of humor.

I know of a number of supermarkets that have set up singles shopping night fund-raisers, where a portion of the proceeds that night go to a charity. And I've heard through the media that many people have met and married as a result of a supermarket shopping trip, though I can't prove it.

I can see it all now. While the men are looking over the gorgeous "tomatoes" in the produce department, the women are checking out the cute "buns" in the bakery. You'll probably meet your mate in . . . where else but . . . the "meet" department.

But as I stated at the outset, the best places to meet other singles is EVERYWHERE, and supermarkets are just another example of what I mean.

Meeting in Nudist Camps

* **Dear George:**

What do you know about nudist camps, as far as their being good places to meet other singles?

I guess it depends on how THOROUGHLY you want to meet them. I personally have never been to a nudist camp (Mother, are you listening?), but I do know several prominent businessmen who married as a result of meeting their mates in a nudist camp. From what I understand, it is very difficult for a single person to even get IN to these camps. For one thing, most camps want to avoid hanky-panky, and they try to keep the ratio of men to women even. Furthermore, they try to be more family oriented, from what I hear.

I heard of one nudist camp that had marble slabs for benches. Whenever people sat down, it sounded like someone applauding.

I once ran a list of questions in my newspaper column addressed to nudists. As far as sitting on marble slabs, I was politely informed that all nudists carry a towel with them and always sit on this towel (okay, so it sounds like people applauding with their gloves on). Here are some of the other questions and answers I received:

Where do nudists keep their loose change, keys, and so on, since they don't have pockets? A man answered that they carry such items in a little "hanging pouch." (Now my next question is, Where does he hang the pouch? Don't answer that!)

What do they do if they don't like volleyball? Do they allow touch football, or is that illegal? One woman replied that it's more fun WATCHING volleyball than playing it. Another said they have all the sports you'd expect to find in any high-class resort. (Oh yeah? I'll bet they don't have ice skating!)

Are they allowed to place a napkin on their laps at mealtime, or is that cheating? Respondents indicated that many nudists dress up for dinner . . . and then undress for dessert.

Is it polite to stare? Not anymore than it is at any other place, I was told.

Are there rules against crossing your legs? No.

When you are introduced to a lady, do you compliment her on her hairdo or what? I was told you should give her a compliment just like you would someone with clothes on. It seems to me you'd be *insulting* the lady if you complimented her on her hairdo, since you obviously would be looking at the wrong place.

When you bump into someone, do you say excuse me or thank you? There were no answers to this one. so I suspect you say thank you.

When I ran this article on nudists, I never realized there were so many "closet" nudists in all sorts of occupations. They all seemed to be pretty good sports, and none of them got mad at me for all the puns I made at their expense. I have to take my hat off to them. (But that's ALL I'll take off!)

Some modern-day nudist camps have condominiums on the premises, where residents live year-around. Most camps are oriented toward families and strictly supervise the people who attend. Many allow first-time visitors to attend with their clothes on to see whether they like it. I understand that most visitors quickly shed their duds once they see everyone else doing it and, subsequently, hardly pay any attention to the nudity.

An amusing note: First-time guests to a nudist camp are referred to as "bunnies," a reference to their unmistakably pink rear ends.

But as far as singles meeting other singles, my guess is you could better spend your time elsewhere, someplace out of the draft, where you'll "catch" more than a cold.

✳ 12 ✳

Meeting on the Internet and Through "900" Telephone Numbers

I PROBABLY SHOULD TITLE THIS CHAPTER the "smart and dumb ways to meet singles," since we'll see a little of both as we read on. But, in any case, meeting singles through the Internet is certainly "smart." (I want to take this opportunity to thank the computer experts who helped me gather the necessary data for this chapter.)

The Internet explosion involves not only hundreds of thousands of businesses but also millions of singles who either place Internet ads or respond to them. In just a few years, it has moved into being the fourth best way to meet other singles. But like everything else, it has both plusses and minuses.

The plusses are that the Internet is very safe and confidential. You can "chat" with thousands of people without giving out your name, address, or anything else that can be traced to you. And it enables you to see a photograph of the person to whom you are "chatting," which personal newspaper ads can't do. Plus you can carry on an instantaneous two-way conversation with another e-mailer for as long as you wish, anywhere in the world, without paying long-distance charges. It really is a marvelous invention.

The minuses are what you find in most media. You can't, for example, be certain that the person you are talking to is really single. Another minus is the number of perverts and pedophiles who are drawn to the Internet because of the anonymity. We read about these sad instances almost weekly in the newspapers. A minus for women is the huge amount of competition they face, since a large majority of personal ads that are placed on the Internet are by women. This could partly be attributed to the fact that there simply are millions more single women than men in the United States. And if you live in a small town, you may hear only from singles who live a far distance away, which can make it difficult or sometimes impossible to arrange a face-to-face meeting.

As most of you know, the most used sites by singles are the chat rooms, the billboards, and the personals. Most of the singles I researched agreed that the chat rooms aren't really the greatest places to meet other singles because too many nonsingles and juveniles constantly butt in and comment on your conversations. It might be fun, but it's not really that practical for singles in the long run.

The billboards are shared by everyone, so your singles message can get buried in a lot of miscellany. I talked to some single people who ran "traveling companion wanted" messages as well as other similar messages on billboards, and they received only a few responses. Billboard messages, as the name implies, are meant to be short and sweet and to the point. But they don't reach a vast number of singles. Thus, they run a distant second to personals.

The personal ads give you the opportunity (in fact they FORCE you) to describe yourself, your background, and your desires. They also enable you to describe in better detail what type of mate you are looking for. They allow you to separate the grain from the chaff as far as the type of person you are looking for. All the research subjects and computer nerds I talked to agreed that the personal ads are the best place for singles to meet on the Internet. So who am I to disagree?

The next question is, Which provider should you use? Most of you already have your own preference as far as your provider is concerned. I checked out a number of them (AOL, Yahoo, Juno, etc., etc.), and they all have thousands—excuse me, hundreds of thousands—of personals for their subscribers. But I didn't want this chapter to end up being a how-to manual, so I settled on only one provider for my research, America On Line. All the research I did was among AOL subscribers, but I don't think the results will be any different with any other provider. So keep an open mind. Even though AOL can be maddeningly slow sometimes, I understand they are launching billions of dollars worth of new satellites to improve their speed.

In order to access the singles "personals" in AOL, you must enter LOVE@AOL.COM! And if you aren't interested in searching out singles from the far corners of the country (or the world), you can zero in on your own geographical area by accessing AOL's DIGITAL CITY NETWORK, or you can enter your town name as your keyword and read ads only from your neighbors.

To help you further reduce the number of ads available for you to scroll through, you can specify your particular desires by entering search words for sex, age, race, hobbies, sports, and so forth, so that you'll only have a few hundred left to peruse.

Now, to even further reduce these hundreds of ads to a more manageable number, you can scroll through just their headlines, and if you find some that are catchy or creative enough to attract you, you can concentrate on them first. That's why it's so important that the headline in your ad be really creative.

Remember the man I researched who used the headline "Dying Millionaire" (see Chapter 8)? Well, another reader got his dying millionaire idea from a previous edition of this book (he really is a millionaire). Within a few weeks, he had e-mail from over three hundred women, all looking to hook up with him. When they brought up his complete personal ad, they saw that it read, "Dying millionaire seeks a trim, attractive lade to save him from dying of boredom." But obviously it still worked, as he received a record number of e-mail responses. He responded to a handful of the ladies, but nothing much came of it. But he and his e-pals had a good time chatting with each other. And he proved beyond a doubt that a catchy headline cuts through the maze and gets results.

Incidentally, in his personal ad, he requested a response from a *slim* lady, along with a photograph. Most concealed the fact that they weren't really slim, and only 32 of the 300 responders included a photograph in their e-mails. As I write this, he's still searching . . . and still bored!

With regard to including photographs in personal ads, I found they are lacking in the majority of them. In checking out 163 personals from women in my geographical area, only 38 included their photos. People who include photos (either imbedded in or attached to their ad) have this fact notated with their headline so that when you scroll through the hundreds of headlines not only the catchy headlines get your attention but also those with the pictorial notation. Thus, if you want your personal ad to be read by a lot more singles, your best bets are to use a catchy headline (two or three words) and include a photo. An old Chinese proverb states, "One picture is worth a thousand words."

Believe me, this is particularly true in personal ads. I know some readers will say they can't afford the cost of a scanner. Well, there are ways around it. I don't want to get into a lot of technical detail, but I understand you can have a friend with a scanner e-mail your photo to you to imbed in your personal ad, or you can use a digital camera or have Kodak photonet e-mail your picture to you for insertion. Or you can have a company such as KINKO's do basically the same thing. The few extra bucks it might cost you will pay off in the vastly increased number of "hits" your personal ad will receive. A lot of people feel that if you don't include your photograph, you must have something to hide, and they won't respond. It's pretty short sighted, but it's still a fact of life. Include a photo with your personal ad and watch the difference in results.

Now for the fun part. What should you say in your personal ad? Fortunately, AOL requests specific information, so all you need do is fill in a lot of blanks. But in several places, you can elaborate more on what type of person you want to hear from. And here's where we get the stereotyped requests. Most of the women state they want a man who is polite, considerate, financially secure, and physically fit; who likes dancing, dining out, traveling, and theater; and who is younger than she is and doesn't hit small children.

Most of the men are equally stereotyped. They usually want a gorgeous, petite, slim, tiny little woman who stays at home and cooks and cleans and beckons to his every whim, and one who will settle for an overweight man considerably older than she is.

That's enough for the dreaming. Now for the reality!

Nearly everyone lies about his or her age. That's no big deal, as long as they chop off only a couple of years.

And nearly everyone lies about his or her weight. Men can easily lop off 30 pounds at the touch of a keyboard. No shame! No guilt! It's the weight they hope to reach if they ever start that diet they've been planning for years. But women are more elusive. If they're concerned about a weight problem, they sidestep it and won't state their weight—in this regard, they are more honest than men. Instead, they'll use terms like *weight and height proportionate, weigh a few extra pounds, slightly overweight, full figured, Rubenesque,* or *it's not what's outside that counts but what's inside.*

All this translated means that she's heavy set. The profile sheet for personal ads on AOL doesn't ask for exact poundage, so most don't bother to list their weights.

The question of weight is the most asked and the most sensitive. But we must remember that some people prefer a mate to be hefty, just as others want him or her to be slim. Honesty is the best policy; sooner or later you're going to have to face the music, and it can be embarrassing to be caught in a lie.

In doing my research for this chapter, I ran several different AOL personal ads. One of them requested, among other things, responses from petite, slim ladies. The first e-mail I received was from a woman on the East coast who was five feet three inches tall and, in her words, "height and weight proportionate." It took me several e-mails to pry out of her that she weighed 163 pounds. That's height and weight proportionate?

I also wanted to test whether there is any danger in being entirely trusting with my respondents, so to four of them, sight unseen, I gave my home telephone number. Two called me back, but

I guess the others thought it so strange that I'd do this that they never called me. Incidentally, one who called me lived a hundred miles away, and we made arrangements to meet halfway for a delightful lunch. She was cute and bubbly and a perfect date. But the fact that she or I would have to drive a hundred miles every time we wanted to get together made further dating futile. This is the only reason I consider e-mail as only the fourth best way to meet other singles. However, for persons living in large towns or metropolitan areas with lots of potential e-mail dates, I would rank it as the second best way to meet singles, right after singles dances and events.

The other respondent who telephoned me in answer to my "slim" personal ad described herself as being "curvy" and said she looks like Mary Tyler Moore (who is very slim). She pushed very hard for us to meet for a few drinks. Her photo on the Internet looked young and pleasant and "slim," so we set up a meeting place. What a surprise I got! She weighed nearly 300 pounds. She explained that she was about to go on a diet and she was a lifetime Weight Watchers member. You just can't trust all the photos displayed on the Internet.

Now let's look at some of the results my research subjects experienced on the Internet. One man placed a short ad on the bulletin board looking for a travel companion. A woman who lived a thousand miles away responded to his ad, and they chatted for a while. After determining that they both seemed compatible, he flew her to his home in Orlando, Florida. Unfortunately, she brought along her 10-year-old son, who was a total terror. The young son caused immediate difficulties and disruptions that the man admitted he couldn't put up with. So the lady responded, "That's okay! We'll visit Disneyworld," which she and her son did. The trip wasn't wasted for them, but it sure was a waste of time and money for the hapless man. Think of how much he could have saved if he had responded only to LOCAL women.

One lady (who only appreciates men with rock-hard butts) asked men for their photos standing up! No one complied. (Several men asked women for their photos standing up and got the same results.)

Another lady responded to a gentleman's personal ad and sent him three pages of e-mail. He was looking for the silent type and he figured she must talk a lot. Nothing came of that one.

One man I talked to thought it was ungentlemanly to ask a woman her weight, but he was exasperated at all the women who beat around the weight bush. So now he requests "dress size" and feels he's being a little more polite. And it sort of catches some of the women off guard; a few of them perhaps think he wants to buy them a garment of some kind, and they readily divulge it. He only continues e-mailing those with small-size dresses.

Another man received e-mail and a photograph from a gorgeous lady. She seemed to meet all his prerequisites and stated that she was looking for a man with a hobby so that she could become interested in his hobby with him. Her photograph in a bikini on a beach was an even bigger enticement. He immediately returned her e-mail with a photo of himself next to one of his expensive antique cars, which was his hobby. He was a good-looking guy, in her age range, but she quickly e-mailed him back that she wasn't interested! Maybe she didn't like his hobby; I don't know! But it seemed a little strange . . . almost as if she simply wanted to see how many responses she could attract that she could turn down—sort of an ego trip.

One lady with her young son moved to the United States from Latvia and couldn't speak English. But she quickly learned the value of the Internet and ran a personal ad on AOL. A gentleman responded, and they eventually made arrangements to meet each other in person. At the meeting, she brought along her young son to interpret for her. End of romance!

I heard a few men claim that some of the women answer their e-mails with a lot of griping and complaining about their past experiences or past husbands, or anything else they can find to be negative about. Naturally, that is the last these women hear from the men. After all, NO ONE wants to get involved with a chronic complainer—male or female! What a waste of good e-mail!

One man, after exchanging a number of e-mail messages with a woman, finally felt guilty and confessed that he was an incurable alcoholic and a woman beater, and she shouldn't have anything more to do with him. She didn't.

A man in his 70s ran a billboard ad looking for a lady to travel with him in his $200,000 RV. As you might expect, all of his 70-year-old respondents inquired whether his motor home had *two* separate bedrooms (with locks on the doors).

One lady who met with several of her e-mail friends reported that the photos they sent to her were at least 10 years old. A few men had the same comment.

Many people, even after a long e-mail relationship, won't disclose their home address. Most just give a post office box, and a few give an office address. This is a good idea; you never really know who is at the other end of your computer. Caution is ALWAYS the best policy.

But, looking to live dangerously, I gave several women my home address and asked them to send me their photos there. They all complied, and I'm still alive, so maybe for most of us it's not that scary a thing. But I still recommend caution, especially among you women!

Meeting on the Internet can be a fun and rewarding experience, and I recommend it to everyone. It's one of the few really smart ways to meet other singles.

Being a glutton for punishment (and to include as many examples as I could in this book), I tried another dating service advertised on television that said I could meet the woman of my dreams. The commercial showed dozens of skimpily clad women in all sorts of beckoning positions, and superimposed over them was the message "FREE CALL"!!

I had to try it. So I called the FREE telephone number on the screen. A sexy-sounding woman welcomed me to her lair and said I could talk to their gorgeous models if I called—guess what—a "900" number! She told me if I called this number now, I'd be connected to the Caribbean island where the orgy was being held. So I got sucked in and dialed the number, having been forewarned that it would cost me $3.99 a minute and that I must be over 18 years of age.

The first voice that came on the phone wasted a lot of my valuable (and costly) time by explaining that I could talk to the woman of my choice by pressing "1" for the orgy room or "2" for the "hot box." Since it was a chilly evening, I pressed "2" for the hot box. A sensuous sounding woman came on the line, welcomed me to the hot box, and listed a few women's names I could date over the phone. I chose to talk to Dominique, the first name they gave me. After a lot of beeping and squeaking and static (at $3.99 per minute), a voice came on and said that there were 146 callers ahead of me waiting to talk to Dominique, and that if I didn't want to hang on until she was free, I could talk to another women on the list. So I selected Donna, and again, after all the costly beeps and static, I was informed that Donna had six callers ahead of me and that I could wait or press a button for another lady. I pressed another phone button and was told my "date" Terry had four callers ahead of me, and so on. I hung up before my phone bill equaled the national debt. I'm willing to bet that there were NO WOMEN available to talk to me or anyone else. They just took advantage of us gullible men and pocketed a sheer profit of $20.

I guess I've proven beyond any doubt that calling "900" numbers to meet a woman is the absolute DUMBEST way to meet other singles!

✳ 13 ✳

Appropriate Behavior for Modern Singles

YOU COULD SAY that the appropriate motto for modern-day singles is "do your own thing" as long as you don't hurt another person or yourself. And while we all must respect a person's upbringing, religious beliefs, and social or familiar mores, I think Victorian customs from that long ago era should be tossed in the ash can, if you are going to make it as a second-time single.

✳ Dear George:

My girlfriend calls men on the telephone all the time. As a lady, I think it's tacky and pushy, and I told her so. Maybe you can correct her.

Maybe instead I should try to correct YOU! What law—religious, social, or moral—says that women can't phone men? Poor Alex Bell must be rolling on this one.

The greatest compliment a man can receive is to have a woman call him on the phone. Just the fact that she cares enough about him to swallow that old-fashioned foolish pride and dial his number is heartwarming. I don't know of any man on earth who deep down doesn't appreciate a woman's call. And modern women call many men as a part of their business duties every day. It's become as normal as breathing.

Let me add *HOWEVER*! If the two of you are single and he already has a steady girlfriend, to call him on a social basis would be intrusive and unwelcome (unless it's an emergency). Also, calling a married man at home for some social reason is taboo (unless business or emergency related).

But other than these few commonsense restraints, call men to your heart's content. We love it! But when you do call, don't complain or gripe about someone or something. A phone call from a lady should be sweet music to our ears.

And don't call a man to check up on who he's going out with or where he went. He doesn't need Big Brother looking over his shoulder (or is it Big Sister?). If the guy is a baseball or football nut, don't call in the middle of the Super Bowl or the World Series games on television. Just a little consideration will go a long way and keep him on the phone a lot longer.

Okay! So you agree to call a man for the first time and you're nervous. What excuse should you use to call him, and what should you say to him? (Some of you liberated women who call men all the time might think this subject belongs to ancient history, but my mail indicates that it is a MAJOR problem still today, with women in their 30s on up. So hang in there!)

As far as an excuse, you don't need an excuse. Just the fact that you want to talk to him is excuse enough. But if you are nervous and need some kind of excuse or "crutch," be creative! Ask him a question relating to his expertise in his business or profession. Ask him how to repair something in your home (you always have something that needs repair). You might even get him to volunteer to come over and handle the repair chore for you; if that happens, consider it an extra bonus. Once you get over the preliminaries, just carry on a simple conversation as you would at the office or if you were out to dinner with him.

I know of a young widow, age 44—I'll call her Linda—who was very interested in getting to know a certain man better, but she couldn't get up the nerve to call him. It was against the way she was brought up, and even though she was 44 years old, she still felt the same way women must have felt in the 1920s. She would NEVER call a man on the phone. Period!

He made it his goal to try to get her to break with this old tradition, so one day he gave a message to her best girlfriend to ask Linda if she could join him for a hike the following day (she liked hiking). He asked that Linda call him to let him know whether or not she could make it. The friend delivered the message, and, after an interminable wait, his phone finally rang. It was Linda, the young widow. Her voice was noticeably shaking, and she sounded like a total nervous wreck. She first started off by apologizing for calling him (a big mistake to apologize) and then told him she was expecting company and couldn't make the hiking date. Sensing how nervous she was, he carried on the conversation like he would with anyone, but it fell on deaf ears. She was more interested in her own nervousness than in what he was saying and completely ignored everything he said. Instead, she blurted out that she should really get out and hike more because she was putting on weight. She asked if he thought 10 pounds overweight was too much. When he replied that some people might say it was too much, she responded, "Well, what are you doing about YOUR weight problem?" (since he was also 10 pounds overweight at the time). What started out as a pleasant conversation ended up as sort of a "you're fatter than I am" name calling match. It was a total disaster, but at least she got some experience in calling a gentleman. Let's hope she learned that a phone conversation should be just the same as talking to a person face-to-face. Be natural and listen to what the other person is saying.

Like I've always said, when calling a man on the phone, the first one is difficult, but the rest are easy. Try it, ladies!

✳ **Dear George:**

We'll use your opinion as a tiebreaker. I took this girl to a lounge, and while I was in the restroom, she struck up a conversation with a strange man at the bar. She didn't even notice when I returned, so after a brief period of being ignored, I walked out, leaving her to converse with her newfound friend. She called me later and said I was rude to have walked out on her. What do you think?

I wouldn't have walked out on her . . . I would have RUN out on her. I think she was the rude one, and it looks like she was using your date as a means of lining herself up with another man. That's the ultimate insult. If a girl accepts a date with a man and he treats her properly, she has an obligation to be his date for the duration of the time, with no side trips.

The only thing I would have done differently is to leave cab fare with the bartender to give her so that I could be sure she would at least get home safely. And I would never see her again unless she learned to be more sensitive to her date's feelings and more trust-worthy. I hope this breaks the tie. (There goes another female reader down the tubes.)

✳ Dear George:

What is your opinion of a man who stands up a woman on a date? My girlfriends seem to have a problem with this.

A person who stands up another person on a date is about the lowest form of life on earth. These creeps are only concerned with themselves and don't have the slightest regard for the other person's time, dignity, or injured feelings. I've been stood up twice, so I know what a terrible feeling it is. It makes you feel hateful and revengeful. It's the pits.

There are only two valid excuses for a person to stand up another person on a date:

1. You are a victim of an auto accident or severe heart attack on the way to the date.
2. You are kidnapped by terrorists and whisked away to Lebanon.

Your girlfriends should spread around the names of the guys who stood them up, as a warning to other potential victims. It'll serve them right.

✳ **Dear George:**

Is a clean bill of health necessary today before intimacies?

Yes, you should be as healthy as possible so you can enjoy it the most. (Just kidding.)

With the spread of AIDS, HIV, and other sexually transmitted diseases, this question is probably on everyone's subconscious whenever they meet a potential Mr. or Ms. Wonderful. Here's a true story, verified by both partners, that really illustrates this concern.

This couple met in an upscale lounge and got along famously all evening long, so much so, that she ended up accompanying him home. She was "hot to trot," but he became leery of her because she seemed like such an "easy mark," especially after she had admitted that she had been "picked up" in a bar once before and lived with the man for 6 months. He was concerned about HER clean bill of health, so the evening passed without anything major happening.

On their next date, she was all over him again, and again he was standoffish for the same reason. Finally, he told her he couldn't get sexually involved with her unless she brought him a letter from her doctor showing that she had tested negative for "those things." He figured he'd probably never hear from her again, and nothing more happened until about 3 weeks later. His lady friend appeared at his door with a lab report from her doctor stating that all "those things" tested negative.

Well, you can guess what happened next. (I think they're still trying to nail the roof of his home back in place.) But the story took an unusual turn soon thereafter. She ran off with her doctor. I guess he also required a clean bill of health.

We all read the newspaper reports showing that the incidence of HIV and AIDS among heterosexuals is spiraling out of control. This should prove that a clean bill of health is definitely a must before intimacies. But it seems to me an awful lot of singles either don't read the newspapers or choose to ignore the facts and figures. My research over the past 2 years shows an alarmingly high number of men and women who "hop in the sack" unprotected on the first or second date, without the slightest concern about the other person's previous sexual adventures. I don't want to sound like an old prude, but it seems like Russian roulette to me. Common sense should dictate that the 30 to 60 minutes of pleasure isn't worth the years and years of pain and agony that accompany HIV and AIDS.

Sorry! I didn't mean to sound like a preacher! It's just that this reckless attitude about catching AIDS seems so prevalent in my surveys that I have become totally alarmed—and maybe you should be as well! Now back to the fun!

✳ **Dear George:**

I want to invite a man to dinner, but I don't know how to do it.

If it's dinner you are preparing in your home, that's easy. Just call him and tell him what you are planning to serve and that you'd like to share it with him. Any single man in his right mind won't need coaxing to accept this invitation. (However, if the dinner menu includes liver, Brussels sprouts, and tripe, get ready for a whopping rejection.) Be reasonably sure he likes the food you will be preparing. Or, better yet, ask what his favorites are and choose one to prepare for him. He'll arrive for dinner with a huge smile on his face.

Now if a woman wants to invite a man to a *restaurant* for dinner, that's a horse of a different color. A good rule of thumb to follow is that the man should do the inviting for dinner in a restaurant. Chances are good that if he wants to dine with you, he'll let you know.

Again, there are exceptions to every rule. If both of you are already very good friends and, for example, it's his birthday or you want to celebrate some special event, then it's okay for the woman to invite the man. And remember! Nothing is more boring for a man (and for a woman, too) than to have dinner with someone you really don't care to spend that much time with, no matter who picks up the tab.

Also, unless it's IRS tax day, April 15th, a time when we're all broke, most men cringe at the thought of a woman paying for the dinner check. It may sound old-fashioned, but don't knock it ladies. It's gotten millions of women billions of dinners.

There are so many other happenings a woman can invite a man to besides dinner, events where both can feel comfortable, such as a walk in the park or on the beach, an artistic event or gallery showing, a condo cocktail party, and so on. There are dozens of these bona fide events to which a woman can invite a man and where he won't feel like he is on the dole.

Now if a couple is in a one-on-one relationship, and they both have flipped over each other, then an occasional dinner on the lady is fine. But I still think it's best to find a good reason for it, such as the anniversary of their meeting or to celebrate a raise at work—something innocuous like that.

Remember! Our manhood is being challenged and assaulted at every turn nowadays. Don't let it happen at the dinner table too!

✳ Dear George:

I must admit we all create our own problems. I met this dynamic man and was attracted to him and felt he liked me also. But our relationship deteriorated after I made a flippant remark in front of his friends. I apologized, but I think it fell on deaf ears. My question is, If you never had a chance to really get to know each other, and you say the wrong thing and still want to see this person, what would be your advice? I feel badly about the situation and hurting someone's feelings.

I know of a similar situation in which this woman really made a blunder that insulted the man she was with. He left in a huff, never expecting to see her again. The following day, she sent him half a dozen roses with a note of apology and followed it up with a personal phone call, again expressing her regrets. Most men can't ignore that kind of sincerity and are bound to give the woman another chance.

The couple in my example is still going strong more than 3 years later, but it never would have been the case if she hadn't made such an impressive apology. It's never too late to start over again.

And even though this question was posed by a woman, the same treatment holds true for a man who messes up his relationship with a woman. The flowers and the *sincere* follow-up apology normally work wonders.

✳ **Dear George:**

I've been hoping for this dreamy guy to ask me out. Finally he called for a date, and I already had one for the same night. I told him I'd take a rain check, but he never called back. Is it okay for me to call him?

Let's face it. He probably feels rejected. Any kind of a "no" answer—even though it was legitimate—is a form of rejection. Some people can accept it better than others.

Many of us get rejected all day long in the business world. If we don't make the sale, it's a form of rejection. If our boss or our client or our customer doesn't like something we say or do, he or she lets us know about it right away—and it's another rejection. In a man's eyes, women are the last hope to save the day—after a day full of rejections That's why it's so important that women avoid the "sound" of rejection when a man asks for a date.

And that trite old remark about the rain check doesn't help matters either. It's worn out.

I think it would have been much better to have said something like this: "I have a prior commitment that I can't get out of, but I'd much prefer to go out with you. Could you instead change the date to another night?" (Mention several alternative nights when you'll be free.)

First of all, this lets him know you really want to go out with him. And then immediately gives him a choice of two or three nights when you are free. That way, you will make him feel comfortable and wanted, not rejected. Chances are, he'll opt for one of your free nights right away, and you'll both be winners.

NEVER tell him that you can't see him because *you have another date with another man*. Make it sound serious—family or business—or you'll kill the whole deal. Here are some other excuses my research has turned up for not accepting a date that are guaranteed to turn most men off:

"I've got to wash my car." (Men think they are more important than your auto's cleanliness.)

"I've got to wash my hair." (Unless you've got hair the length of Crystal Gayle's, most men think you can get up a little earlier the following morning to wash it.)

"I've got to help my kids with their homework." (Until what hour? And why didn't you help them sooner, before it got to such a crisis stage?)

"I'm going out with my girlfriend." (To do what? Look for other men?)

"I'm too tired." (Would you say that if Leonardo DeCaprio called for a date?)

Ladies, be a little imaginative in the way you drop us poor guys, even if you have to tell a little white lie to spare our feelings. It's so important. After all, we're just a bunch of little boys trying to cope in a woman's world.

As for phoning the man in this letter, do it by all means. He showed he was interested in you. Now it's your turn to show you are interested in him.

✳ Dear George:

Why don't you tell your female readers not to wear a ring on their wedding finger if they want to attract single men. Several times I have bypassed some really nice-looking women because they looked like they had a wedding ring on, only to discover later—and too late—that they were single.

Agreed! Most single men—unless they don't mind looking down the barrel of a shotgun held by a jealous husband—will steer clear of married women and those who appear to be married. Some single women, such as waitresses and others who serve the general public, find it necessary to wear a phony wedding ring to discourage the would-be mashers. But there are plenty of other single gals who wear an ornamental ring on their wedding fingers that could easily be misconstrued as a wedding ring, or at least an engagement ring.

(Speaking for myself, whenever I have a date with a really "great" gal who happens to wear a ring on her wedding finger, I never mention it to her. I figure that it keeps the competition from "hitting on her," and therefore, I know she'll be more readily available whenever I call. Sneaky, eh?)

Ladies! If you are in the market for a man, keep your wedding ring finger as bare as a hound's tooth . . . until Mr. Wonderful rings it for you.

✳ Dear George:

How long do you think is a reasonable time to be going with a man before marriage is considered?

Why get married and spoil a good friendship?

Of course, there is no possible time frame for determining when marriage is right for you. However, your age plays an important part. If you are 14 years old, you've got all the time in the world. On the other hand, if you are 95, better get that ring in a hurry.

I think more important than how long it should take is how much you know about the other person. I know of so many second-, third-, and fourth-time newlyweds who discovered too late that they didn't know enough about their marriage partners—about his drinking problem, or her infidelity, or his temper, manners, habits, and so on.

The most important thing you can do is to take the time to see your potential mate under all different types of situations BEFORE you tie the knot. Put away your rose-colored glasses and pay attention to him or her in everyday situations that you will encounter when married. It helps avoid not only the trauma of divorce, but also the double trauma of attorneys' fees. The old adage still holds true: Act in haste, repent at leisure.

✳ **14** ✳

Understanding Single Men

I DON'T THINK you ever can thoroughly understand a single man, unless you find a way to dig deep into his psyche to find out what type of person he really is, and what his thoughts really are. It's very difficult to do. I think the best a woman can do is associate with him long enough so that his deep down feelings and persona eventually come somewhat nearer to the surface.

I have talked with many women who thought they had met their Mr. Wonderful, only to discover too late that he wasn't anything at all like they first judged him to be. After they had associated with the man over a period of time, they discovered his real persona, and they didn't like what they saw. So ladies, don't jump to conclusions until you associate with your man over a longer period of time. My guess is that it takes a *minimum* of 6 months of closeness before you start to really know your man.

Conversely, don't jump to negative conclusions about a man either. Unless he's a real out-and-out slob, get to know him better before you make your final judgment. I heard from a woman who upon meeting a man for the first time stated emphatically that he wasn't her type. She was in her 40s and he was in his 50s. Her dislike for him centered more around the cosmetic than substantive reasons. She didn't like his facial features, his weak chin, his sagging stomach. She couldn't find anything right with him, and she tended to give him the cold shoulder.

However, he continued to pursue her. One day just to get him off her case, she agreed to join him on his sailing yacht for a Sunday cruise. While they sailed on his rather large boat, he expected her to act as first mate and barked orders for her to perform certain chores with the riggings while he manned the tiller. She found herself taking directions and orders from him and thoroughly enjoying it. Before she realized it, she began to respect his ability as a leader, as a captain, and as a man who knew what he was doing. In no time, she completely forgot about his weak chin and sagging stomach and fell head over heels in love with him. And on subsequent voyages, she became a rather good first mate, too, all the while adoring her captain.

When I last heard from her, she stated that she was deeply in love with the guy, more so than she had even been with her ex-husband when they were first married. If she had stuck with her original feelings, she never would have experienced the thrill of falling in love.

Single men set up so many barriers around them that even they get confused and lost. You've got to get to know most men much better before you toss them aside as being incompatible.

✳ Dear George:

Men will ask me for my telephone number to call for a dinner date and then never call. Why don't they call? Is it just to make me feel they are not anxious?

Judging from the amount of mail I get on this subject, it seems to be a big problem with single women. In my book, a man who tells you he is going to call and doesn't, after a reasonable length of time, has one of two basic problems. Either he isn't very creative and, therefore, doesn't know how to end a date with anything except a false promise, or, more likely, he figures he has you "hooked" and is now putting you on the shelf with all his other possessions. He'll probably call you someday in the distant future, when it suits his particular situation or when he can't get a date from someone else.

Unless you don't mind being used as a doormat by this person, scram!

The next time a man tells you he will call you soon, PIN HIM DOWN! Ask him when he thinks he'll call so you can be sure to be home when the phone rings. If he hems and haws, it probably means he doesn't plan to call you, so drop it (and him) and move on. Don't waste your time with false hopes.

Usually men on an ego trip will give the "I'll call you soon" rubbish with no intention of following through. If you know your date is on such a trip, try this just for the fun of it (and to be a little bit nasty). When he says that he'll call you soon, tell him he needn't bother and immediately change the subject. He'll probably beg you for a chance to call you, if for no other reason than to save his bruised ego.

A man with a semblance of courtesy, who doesn't plan to go out with you on a regular basis, will usually thank you for a nice time (it's probably a lie) and wish you good luck on your job, or in your new home, or something of that nature and let it go at that. In other words, he'll be polite without giving you false hopes.

Conversely, if a man has enjoyed being with you, he'll have his own special way of letting you know it and you'll probably hear from him again real soon. The safe way is not to read anything into what he says until he follows through on it.

One last thing: If you have been getting a lot of men putting you off like this, maybe it's YOUR fault. If you are too cold or aloof on a date, the guy probably figures it will take until he's 99 years old to warm you up, and it's not worth it. Or if you are the clinging vine type, gushing all over him, the distant sound of wedding bells may scare him off. Check yourself out. And while you're at it, check out your appearance in a full-length mirror.

Finding Mr. Wonderful is a science, not an art.

✳ **Dear George:**

Why do men go to singles dances and not ask women to dance? What are they there for?

Many men are basically shy when it comes to women. Women don't believe this, but it's true. Many men just can't get up the nerve to ask a strange woman to dance. Many can't even ask one they've known for a while because they feel they aren't good enough as far as dancing ability is concerned. I think women have attached so much importance to a man's dancing capabilities that men are intimidated unless they actually know they are great dancers.

I ran a survey among single men, asking them if they felt comfortable asking a strange woman to dance. A whopping 75 percent said they feel *uncomfortable* asking a strange woman for a dance. However, all said they probably would dance with a strange woman if SHE gave the impression that she was interested in meeting them.

Most of the men I surveyed said they can't face being rejected. Others said the women make it look as though they are waiting for their dates to arrive. Almost half said they felt they weren't a good enough dancer compared to the men "she" had already danced with that evening. And half said they only dance the slow dances, and when one comes along, the woman is usually besieged with other dance partners and it's too late.

I've got an idea for you women readers: Instead of always *dying* to dance, why not instead just strike up a conversation with a man and don't push him into dancing. After he gets to know you a little better and he feels more comfortable, he'll ask you to dance. Be patient.

✳ **Dear George:**

I met a man I was interested in, and he in me. I guess I made a mistake admitting I found him attractive because he then pursued and pressured me sexually until I realized our friendship was not going to progress at all until we got over the sexual hurdle. I finally gave in to him, and that was my second mistake. From that point on, he assumed I was HIS girl, and he started making all kinds of plans for the future, in addition to being extremely possessive and jealous. It was impossible to make him understand the reality of the situation, i.e., that although everything he was offering sounded very nice, I was still trying to get to know him better first. And although I was very fond of him so far, I still had made no commitment. Attempting to explain it to him was useless. He just couldn't comprehend it, and sadly, the relationship ended. Due to his obsession, he could not handle just being friends. He was essentially my first venture into the dating scene since my divorce. Is it a mistake for a woman to admit that she is attracted to someone? Will sex, or the absence of it, always be a block to getting to know someone better? Does having sex imply a commitment? HELP! What are the rules today?

Doctor Ruth! Where are you when I need you?

I think possessiveness and jealousy have ruined more relationships than anything else, and yours apparently is no exception. On the other hand, some people go out of their way to make their partners jealous, and they end up getting what they deserve.

I don't think it's a mistake to admit to someone that you are attracted to him. In fact, I think it's a necessity to let him know how you feel as soon as you have those feelings. If you don't, you're playing games with the guy, and game players always lose. However, once he knows your feelings, if he starts to become possessive or take you for granted, then at least you've learned a lot about him early on and can make a better judgment about whether or not to continue seeing him before you waste too much of your time or get involved any deeper.

By the way, as far as your question about sex, if sex doesn't imply some amount of love and commitment, then isn't it called "promiscuity"?

The rules today are the same as they've always been . . . they're just more out in the open and discussed more freely. Let your conscience be your guide and resist being badgered into doing something you don't want to do or don't feel comfortable with. Any *gentleman* will respect you for it.

✳ **Dear George:**

You printed a letter from a man about possessive women and his complaints on the subject. Now I want to complain about men, especially self-centered men. Do you realize how boring it is for women on a date to listen to you men telling us what YOU want, YOUR opinions, goals, ideas, ad nauseam. You men kill any chance of a relationship by being so self-centered and talking about YOU all the time.

The Bible tells us that Samson killed 20 thousand Philistines with the jawbone of an ass. I suspect that just as many relationships have been killed with the same weapon, if you get my drift.

The problem is that self-centered people—men and women— don't realize they are this way and how boring they really are. They are talking about their favorite subject—themselves—and to them that's sheer enjoyment and excitement.

It's too bad that more people can't take the hint. When a person will only go out with you one time and no more, you should immediately check your breath, your deodorant, or your conversation.

✳ **Dear George:**

When you accept a drink from a strange man in a bar, does he expect something in return?

You can bet your sweet bippie he does! At the least he expects some conversation in return. At the most? . . . well!

If a man buys you a drink and bypasses the less attractive gals in the lounge, there's perhaps a spark of romantic interest lurking in that drink, and it's aimed directly at you. It's his mating call!

When you accept his drink, you usually must also plan to accept at least some chitchat from him no matter how boring it might become. I'm not saying this is all bad. I know lots of great friendships that started this way. But if you happen to get stuck with a real bore whom you can't easily shake, it makes it a mighty expensive drink for you.

If you ever find yourself in such a position in which you can't get rid of the guy, try this: Look at your wristwatch and remark, "I can't understand what's keeping my fiancé. He had a late meeting at the Sheriff's department, where he works, but he should be off duty by now."

End of mating call!

On the other hand, if this guy buys a round for everyone at the bar, that's a different story. He's probably being overly generous, celebrating some accomplishment, or showing off his wealth. If this often happens in places where you go, let me know. I've got a whole bunch of freeloading friends waiting to frequent your lounge.

✳ **Dear George:**

Why are so many of you men neurotic?

Maybe it's because we have nothing better to do.

✳ **Dear George:**

How right you were when you said in one of your columns, "Act in haste, repent at leisure." I just finished a whirlwind courtship in which the man who swept me off my feet had visions of sugarplums dancing in my head. We both were in our mid-40s and although I had only known him a month, we were already talking engagement, marriage, honeymoon. I was so blinded by it all that I never got to know what kind of a person he really was. All I could think of was that my search had ended. Luckily, I didn't lose anything more than my heart (and that will mend). Once I opened my eyes and saw the kind of person he was deep down, I knew I could never put up with what I saw and learned, and our relationship ended. I am now repenting at leisure. Next time I'll heed your advice from the start.

Enough said. But be sure you don't make the next guy pay for the last guy's mistakes.

✳ Dear George:

What did I do wrong? I went with this man half a dozen times and we got along great . . . and I mean really great! He let me know he cared, and just as things were going really well, he abruptly stopped seeing me. He hasn't returned my calls or a note I wrote him. I hear he tells everyone how much he likes me, but I can't get a peep out of him. What gives?

I don't think you did anything wrong. It looks to me like you got a scared "jack rabbit" who is now hiding in his den, reveling at how lucky he was to escape capture by a "fox." Chances are he's been divorced once or twice and is very leery of getting involved again. This happens to a lot of singles. I do think he should at least have the decency to return your phone calls or drop you a note, but maybe this tells you how scared he really is. He's sort of burying his head in the sand, hoping these serious thoughts he's having will just fade away. It sounds to me like you almost landed him.

I know that most gals would say to drop him like a hot potato, but I say to hold on a little longer. If you have planted a seed, you have to keep watering it if it's ever going to flower. I'd drop him a short note—not gushy or demanding—just friendly, wondering what's happening in his life. I'd write one every 3 or 4 weeks, so as not to appear pushy. If you can, try to be seen with other men at parties or functions that he or his friends might attend (the old jealousy bit). Try it for 3 months or so and see what happens. If nothing happens, then maybe the seed turned out to be a weed. It happens!

✳ Dear George:

Why is it that the only thing you men think of is sex? Can't you just have a good time?

It's not true that all we ever think about is sex. We spend at least an hour a day thinking about something else. (Just kidding, Mom!)

And it might surprise you to know that many people—men and women—think sex is having a good time. Usually the women who complain the most about men and sex never have either one. Judging from the rest of your letter (which I mercifully spared my readers from), you sound like you are only interested in seeing the bad side of men. The women who have the best relationships with men are those who treat men as they themselves wish to be treated . . . in a pleasant, positive, considerate manner, not always looking for faults. Try it! You might even have a good time yourself someday.

✳ **Dear George:**

How do you keep a man interested in you if you don't want to go to bed with him on the first date?

Have two dates with him the same day. (Just fooling. See the next letter.)

✳ **Dear George:**

How can you keep a man interested long enough to give yourself time to decide whether you want a sexual relationship with him?

If that's the ONLY thing on his mind, you're probably better off letting him move on. But if both of you are exploring a long-term relationship, he'll appreciate you for being cautious, open, and frank with him. Tell him how you feel and that you just don't get involved unless you know that the man is right for you.

Most men will appreciate the fact that you aren't "easy" and will really like you better for it. However, be sure you don't make it sound like you are only interested in hearing the sound of wedding bells, or you might scare him away before you ever get started. Here's the best advice to follow: When in doubt, be totally honest.

✳ **Dear George:**

Here I am alone, thinking of my dates this past year. A few I chose not to see again, but more chose not to see me a second time. The men made it very clear that intimacy (sex) should be a conclusion of the date. I felt that I did not know the men well enough, and I did not feel the desire for such closeness after one date. Some women have told me that men have implied before asking for a date that sex—or I should say "making love"—would be part of it. So, I have had some great "one dates." I feel that making love would not have brought me a closer friendship. What do you think?

Where do you gals meet these guys? In the city dump? I think I know eight or nine thousand single men, and 99.9 percent of them are super guys, not the frustrated, hard up sex fiends some of you readers seem to describe. Besides, what ever happened to the famous women's intuition? If you put it to use, you won't end up in these situations. In answer to your question about whether making love to someone you hardly know will bring you a closer friendship, there's a good chance it's going to bring you a whole lot more than "friendship," if you know what I mean. Tell these creeps to get lost!

✳ **Dear George:**

How do you turn down a man who asks you to dance and then accept another man's offer minutes later, without insulting the first man?

Life sure gets complicated, doesn't it? Let's face it! When you turn down a man, you've already insulted him somewhat. And by accepting another man's invitation a few minutes later, you add injury to insult. Normally, the first man will take the hint (and hate you for the rest of his life, probably). But to avoid hurt feelings, when you turn down a man, maybe you should say that you are just not in a dancing mood right now and thank him for asking you. Then, when you accept another man, it could be interpreted that your "dancing mood" has changed, giving the first man a chance to salvage some of his ego.

It's refreshing to see that someone is interested in avoiding hurting another's feelings. I've seen plenty of instances in which the women couldn't care less about the man's feelings.

✳ **Dear George:**

When a lady is asked to dance and then the man proceeds to make vulgar moves on the dance floor, what is the best way to show disapproval of such behavior, other than simply walking off the floor? I am a very affectionate person and enjoy dancing very much. But the dance floor is not the place for suggestive and pawing actions. I know of no women who find this complimentary. I wonder if this type of male is only capable of performing on a dance floor. What is the male point of view?

Probably most people—male and female—would suggest that you stuff barbed wire down his shorts. Of course, you should walk off the dance floor, and ignore the jerk completely.

One "creep" can ruin it for a hundred nice guys, so be sure you don't fall into the trap of judging everyone else by the actions of one person.

And before you women become overly smug, I'm sure for every guy who is a creep, there's probably a woman who is the same (a "creepette"?). I know of plenty of instances in which the gals have been just as suggestive on the dance floor and even worse. I also know of several instances in which women have followed perfect strangers home from a lounge unbeknownst to the men, because the women "wanted to get to know them better." I guess before we condemn one gender, we should accept the fact that both sexes share the blame equally. Like the old saying goes, "What's sauce for the goose is sauce for the gander." (But who wants a sauced goose?)

✳ **Dear George:**

I've read your column for several years, and I always seem to notice that your letters from women complain about men attacking them on the dance floor, etc. Don't you ever get letters from men complaining about women? What bothers me the most is women who have too much to drink and then try to force us to dance with them.

I've had them actually drag me onto the dance floor; if I didn't go along with them, I would have lost a shirtsleeve. This has happened more than once. Say something for the men for a change.

I agree with you wholeheartedly. I'm sure that every man has nearly lost an arm—or a wristwatch—trying to pull away from a tipsy lady who must dance at all costs. And if you are successful in pulling away and avoiding her, she'll be the first to spread the story that you are conceited or antisocial or some such rubbish. She usually ends up ruining the evening for you so that you leave earlier than planned.

Ladies, if a man wants to dance with you, he'll ask, unless it's a ladies choice dance. If you get a bashful one and feel you have to do the asking, fine! But don't force the issue into an embarrassment for the both of you. Let's face it! Like it or not, some men don't enjoy dancing.

＊　**Dear George:**
How do you handle those rejecting "nos" from men?
That's a switch! Usually it's us men who hear the "nos!"

To avoid getting a "no" answer, why not follow the rules of good salesmanship? A good salesman never asks a question in such a way that he can get "no" for an answer He instead usually offers a choice of something or something, instead of a choice of yes or no. Maybe you can work this into whatever it is you've been asking them.

Here are a few examples of offering a choice of something or something, rather than a choice of yes or no:

"Would you care to dance to this tune, or would you rather wait for a slower one?" (You give two choices that can't be answered with a no!)

"Would you care to join me for dinner on a weekday, or is the weekend better?" (Again, a choice of something or something.)

"Your place or mine?" (How can he refuse?)

✳ **Dear George:**

This man I've known for several years asked me to marry him several months ago. I told him I'd have to think about it and put him off. Now he hardly sees me anymore and has never mentioned marriage since. Did I goof?

Probably one of the most important tips I can give the ladies is this: If a man asks you to marry him, you'd better accept him right away. If you give him time to think about it and reconsider his proposal, he's probably not going to ask you again, at least not right away. It's not that he doesn't love you as much or anything like that. Men usually just look for an excuse to reconsider this big step, and in many cases, it's all downhill from there.

Here's something my research turned up about lots of men. Once they start to get some serious marriage thoughts in their mind about a particular woman, some sort of "bachelor survival instinct" takes over, causing the man to suddenly notice all the faults the woman has so that he can feel justified in talking himself out of these marriage thoughts. I call these "escape hatches."

Ladies! If you have a man who you think is ready to pop the question, be on your utmost best behavior. Naturally, don't become a fake or don't be misleading, but walk around on "egg shells" while he has these matrimonial thoughts in his head. Don't notice other men. Don't argue or complain. Don't voice negative feelings. Be as sweet as you can possibly be. Chances are he'll only be in this marriage mood for a very short time, so don't do anything to disturb it. DON'T GIVE HIM ANY ESCAPE HATCHES!

✳ **Dear George:**

Where do you find young, rich, good-looking women?
Usually on the arms of young, rich, good-looking MEN!

15

Understanding Single Women

FIRST OF ALL, let me state unequivocally that any man who says he understands women is the biggest fool on the face of the earth. NO ONE can understand women, not even other women. Just when you think you've figured them out, they do a complete flip-flop, and you're back to square one. I guess it's this mystery and mystique that keeps us men coming back for more.

But ain't it great!

✳ Dear George:

I've entered a new phase in my life. I finally feel like a seasoned single person. I have felt desired, rejected, superior, inferior, confident, uncomfortable, lonely, happy to be alone, restless, and peaceful. I have learned to come out of the married shell. I am more conscious of my appearance and conversation. I am less domestic, more artistic and creative. I feel braver. I can handle tasks easier. I make my own decisions. I am more assertive, and sometimes it makes me appear a bit selfish and self-centered. There is excitement in the air . . . adventure awaits me.

I am now a grown-up SINGLE WOMAN!

What a nice way to start a hard-to-write chapter about understanding women. Thanks for the pleasant thoughts.

At first when I contemplated this chapter, I was tempted to just print the masthead and leave the following 10 pages blank, to show that we don't or can't begin to understand women, especially single women. But then I took another look at my files full of letters from women and discovered that they seemed to expose women's thoughts and feelings (though just barely). So I thought maybe some of you single men might be able to glean a little bit of information about the innermost workings of womanhood that might help you in the future.

God help you!

I once received a letter from a woman in her late 30s who happened to live in the same city. She was new to the area and wrote that she couldn't get up enough nerve to attend any of the numerous singles events that were going on, even though there was a wide variety of functions to choose from. She also mentioned that she didn't have a job, and was at a loss as to where to start looking, and would appreciate any help I could give her.

I called her on the telephone soon after receiving her letter and suggested that we meet and put our heads together to help work out a solution for her and get her off to a flying start in her new city. She readily agreed to it, and we scheduled a meeting for 1:00 P.M. the following day at a public place that she suggested. I gave her a phone number to call in case she had a change of plans.

Then, on my own, without her knowledge, I invited two of the town's most eligible bachelors to join us after 1:30 P.M., sort of as a surprise encounter. One of the men had a few job openings in his business and said that he would be happy to discuss them with her. I thought it would be a friendly gesture and make her feel more welcome to the city. Also, it would give her the opportunity to get to know three bachelors who were all gentlemen and thoroughly aboveboard. Then, if she ever did decide to attend a singles function in the future, she would at least know us, since we all attended most of them, and we could help introduce her to other people with interests similar to hers.

In addition, as an extra benefit, she might qualify for employment from one of my friends, if her job credentials met his job requirements. It felt good knowing that I'd helped someone I hadn't even met. I was sure it would be a pleasant afternoon.

So guess what happened?

I showed up on time! My two bachelor friends showed up on time! BUT SHE NEVER SHOWED UP!

Nor did she call the number I gave her. Many years have gone by since this incident, and I still haven't received a letter or an excuse or an apology or anything from her. I guess I can conclude that I was just plain stood up! And so were my two bachelor friends, who, by the way, will never do this favor for me again.

The thing that bugs me the most is that I went out of my way to be a good friend to someone I'd never seen or met, and I got left holding the bag—not even a phone call or short note. I can't believe it!

You women who think you have troubles understanding men, top THAT one!

✳ **Dear George:**

I'm one of those shy, single ladies, and whenever I attend a singles party, I tend to meet maybe one person and visit the entire evening with that one person . . . and it's usually some woman I already know. Females feel uncomfortable going up to a man and starting a conversation. And if the man is new at this too, well . . . no one will meet anyone. Got any ideas?

Yes! I'm going to bawl out the majority of single women. When you attend anything where there are lots of singles in attendance, you usually hightail it for a dimly lit table way back in the far corner of the room and sit with one or two other women. And when the evening is over, you're usually the first ones to complain that you didn't meet any men and had a lousy time. I've seen and heard it a thousand times.

What man in his right mind is going to fight all the way back to the far reaches of the room to where you and your girlfriends are happily carrying on a conversation, and then try to break up this happy ensemble with his own conversation or dance request? It ain't going to happen!

And when you sit at a table—any table—you are going to miss out on meeting half of the people in the room or more. Men don't feel comfortable going around a room trying to break up matched sets of women who seem perfectly happy and content carrying on their conversations with their women friends.

GET AWAY FROM THE TABLES AND GET OFF YOUR DUFFS! Wear some comfortable shoes and stand up for at least the early part of the evening. And if you have to sit, do so at the front of the room so that you are accessible to all. The most successful singles parties I have ever run were those in which I had hundreds of singles in attendance and furnished only 10 tables and approximately 50 chairs. I FORCED everyone to mingle and move around and dance—especially dance. The shy men figure that as long as they have to remain on their feet, they might as well do it more comfortably on the dance floor. It worked every time.

Naturally, I have heard complaints from the dyed-in-the-wool "table sitters," but the success ratio of people who met and developed serious relationships as a result of my parties more than overcame the spate of complaints.

Now ladies, let me divert for a minute. Since this chapter discusses women and how to understand them, I have a question to ask, sort of an "author's prerogative." When two women get together in a restaurant, in a lounge, at a dance or a party, or ANYWHERE for that matter, WHAT DO YOU FIND TO TALK ABOUT ALL THE TIME? Whenever I see two women together, they are ALWAYS totally engrossed in conversation with each other, even though they may have been together all day or all week! Don't you gals ever run out of things to talk about? You always appear interested and excited about your conversations and never look bored! After hours and hours of chatting, what's left to say?

I know when two MEN get together under similar circumstances, we run out of things to say in about 10 minutes or so, and then our conversation drifts to a discussion of who is the best looking gal in the room, or some other "enlightening" topic along those lines.

I asked a lovely lady named Theresa what she and her girlfriends talk about so much! I finally pinned her down. The topics of their conversations include discussing old and new friends, and trashing a few of them, situations at work and at home, clothes and stupid outfits worn by others, guys who are cute, dance bands they like and dislike, things they like and dislike about men, ways for women to rule the world, and animal rights. And if they're in a lounge that offers dancing, "girl talk" allows them to appear more interested in their conversation than in the men around them and, thus, less like an easy "pick up."

If she's the average woman, we men now at least have a clue about how to break up these "matched sets" and start a conversation of our own with one of them. Here's an idea: Approach one of the women whom you find attractive and bet her a dance that you can name one of the subjects that she and her friend have been discussing all evening long. She'll probably accept your challenge, so then tell her one of the subjects Theresa listed in the previous paragraph. If she's honest and admits it, you've got yourself a dancing partner for the next dance. And if she denies they talked about any of these subjects, so what? Ask her for the dance anyhow! You've broken the ice, and that's what they're really there for in the first place.

Theresa told me so!

✳ **Dear George:**
You told women not to give out their phone numbers and addresses to new acquaintances, and now that's messing it up for us men. They're using you as their reason for not giving them out.

Hooray! Let's face it: Women are becoming more clever and more careful. They're only giving out pertinent information to those they know and trust. That's the way it should be, what with all the creeps on the loose these days. It's the only safe way to go, and you should respect them for it.

Did it ever dawn on you that maybe these women really don't want you to call them and they're just using me as an excuse?

✳   **Dear George:**

Why don't you tell your female readers that men don't like possessive women.

One of the biggest complaints in the singles world—and I've heard it from men by the score—is that some women tend to became possessive after two or three dates, sometimes after one date! I'm sure men do, too, but that's another chapter. We're only raking *women* over the coals in this chapter.

It's worth repeating that possessiveness wrecks more potential relationships than any other single factor, in my book. Sometimes a woman seems to think that because she and her date had a good time together, and he whispered sweet nothings in her ear, that he is HERS. I've heard that some women even start to make plans for his weekend activities or begin to expect him to *account for his time* spent apart. Many think he shouldn't date other women. In short, she suddenly "owns" him.

This possessiveness is man's greatest fear, and it automatically triggers a defensive reaction in which he subconsciously overly asserts his independence, and the whole relationship goes down the tubes.

Gals! The only time you really can think that you OWN the guy is when you're both standing before a preacher and you've got a "you-know-what" license in your hip pocket.

And even then, don't take this ownership for granted.

✳   **Dear George:**

I've gone with a girl for 7 months. I take her to dinner, dancing, sports, etc., and we have a very good time together. However, when I take her home, she suddenly becomes as cold as an ice cube. I've always treated her as a gentleman should, and maybe that's my problem.

I think SHE has the problem, not you. Some people are "givers" and some are "takers." Sounds to me like you've got a real "taker," and she seems to be taking YOU for granted. Life is too short. Move on!

And continue to be a gentleman. Most women appreciate it.

Here are two letters I received—one from a woman and the other from a man—that show how maladjusted some people can become out there in singles-land. Both of the writers seem to me totally into themselves, and such people usually can only get "losers" for dates. As far as I'm concerned, they got what they deserved. Read on!

✳ Dear George:

I was married for 30 years (true blue). Suddenly, my husband left me for a much younger woman. I am an attractive, intelligent, outgoing woman. Seeking friendly companionship, I decided to try some singles social events. What a put-down! I found (probably the result of the ratio of single men to women) that the 50- to 60-year-old men at each event gravitated to the 35- to 45-year-old women, leaving us 45- to 55-year-olds sitting like undiscovered wallflowers.

When I was finally asked to dance at one event, I was held in a body lock suitable for points in any wrestling match. Moreover, when I pulled back, I was called a cold fish by possibly the rudest man I've ever met. Having just begun, I quit!

I'll stay home before I'll subject myself to such demeaning treatment again. I'm not as desperate as all those pot-stomached, hair-receding Romeos seem to think all us gals sitting on the sidelines are.

Some of us—I dare say many—are modest, caring, respectable mothers and grandmothers who would much rather be home making popcorn and watching old movies on TV but for some reason or other have found ourselves seeking the company of others. Personally, I think many of you (50-ish) fellas are missing the boat. We (50-ish) women are not after your money (we have our own). We don't need your security (we are secure). You don't have to dress and act like you are 30-ish (we like 50-ish). We understand going to bed early (for rest). Now if by chance, after reading this, some of you men decide to ask us to dance, please remember you are probably holding someone's mother in your arms.

Show a little respect.

Just had to blow off some steam. Thanks for listening.

Whew!!!! There's more!

✳ Dear George:

I've had it with modern-day single women. I have never met more rude, inconsiderate women in my life. Of the four women I recently made dates with, one stood me up cold, no explanation, nothing! One broke four dates in a row, including dinner and theater, with tickets in hand. One broke two out of three dates (left a message 3 hours prior to date time on my answering machine). One left a message on my answering machine 2 hours before our date saying, "Something came up!" All this was in a 30-day period. The broken dates were not just simple "find something to do" evenings. I had made many preparations.

I started asking myself, "What's the matter with you? Ugly? Masher? Womanizer?"

My friends say I'm a nice guy and that I have class, money, looks, and respect for women.

If a woman isn't sure she can be there, she shouldn't make a date. If a true emergency comes up that causes her to break a date, she shouldn't rely on a cold answering machine to relay the reason. She should personally tell her date the reason. To the women who wonder why some men take you out, get what they want, and dump you, they probably were at one time a nice guy like me who got tired of being shoved around.

Boy, what a lot of garbage! If you can't swim, grab a chandelier! It seems to me we're sinking into a sea of ego trips and self-pity with these two people. It's too bad they're from different cities; they sound like they'd make an excellent pair. I can see them on a date now, sitting alone on a moonlit night, complaining about how bad everyone else is (except themselves, of course). Both of these writers are being grossly unfair by condemning all singles for the actions of a few. I hear this same junk 20 times a day.

I know of a thousand great singles for every jerk—male and female. And speaking for the pot-stomached, hair-receding men among us, I object to the woman's discriminating description.

Many of us male singles are FATHERS who deserve the same respect she claims she deserves as a mother. Her bitterness toward men is obvious, probably brought to a head as a result of her husband leaving her for another woman (or did he escape?). She seems to forget it was HIS action, not ours. Give the rest of us a break, lady, and back off!

As far as the self-pitying male on his own ego trip, I agree that anyone who stands up another person is lower than a worm's kneecaps. But he had *seven* dates in 1 month that were canceled by the gals. In this day and age, when we have such a large plurality of single women over single men, he set a world's record for canceled dates. I don't think he should waste his time wondering what's wrong with women. I think he should instead worry about what's wrong with HIM.

However, things always work out for the better. He can spend the money he saved from these seven canceled dates on a good shrink. It might be the best investment he'll ever make.

And while he's at it, he should get rid of that telephone answering machine. Maybe he'll get more dates if they can't cancel them.

✳ **Dear George:**

I was married for 25 years and am now divorced. I am 45 years old, love to dance, and adore men. I have gone to several singles dances and happy hours. My problem is that for some reason it seems the only men interested in me are in their 60s. They are very nice, but I don't feel comfortable with the age difference, and I would much prefer meeting someone my own age.

It seems the men my age are only interested in "pretty young things." By the way, even though I'm a mother, I love to be held close while dancing. The gal who wrote you that letter can stay home in front of the TV by herself.

Obviously, this letter was written in response to the letter printed on the preceding pages (by the woman who was put into a wrestling body lock while dancing). The nice thing about this column writing business is that when we get depressed by an extremely negative letter writer, we get picked right back up again by nice, positive thinking, lovely people.

Now, if we can only figure out a way for this letter writer to be noticed at parties by 45-year-old men . . . hmmmm!

Lady! How are you at handstands?

☀   **Dear George:**

Why do most men expect the woman to do the laundry and cleaning, even when she is working full-time also?

Why send an amateur to do a pro's work? I presume you are married, so what the heck is this doing in a singles book?

Oh well! Let's look at it from a husband/wife angle, just for a breather. You mentioned the old female complaint of having to do the laundry. If you have to take your wash to the Laundromat, then I agree it's an inconvenience. And if you have to beat your clothes clean with rocks on the bank of a stream, then it's definitely a hassle. But the gals I have heard complain the most about doing laundry have an automatic washer and dryer. What's the big deal?

In my married days, I was led to believe laundry was a horrible chore. But now that I've done my own laundry for a dozen years, I've found it's really no big deal.

First you toss the clothes into the washer (along with assorted loose change, a wallet or two, and a Bic that soon won't flick anymore) and wait for the buzzer to sound. Then you toss the whole mess into the dryer and wait for another buzzer. Big deal! Total actual work time involved—3 minutes. And since all the clothes are wash and wear, you simply stuff them into drawers and voilà! The whole chore is completed.

Now about the other complaint about cleaning the house. Usually the male partner cuts the grass and cares for the exterior of the house and does all the manual, menial labor inside and out. I'll bet by the end of the year, if you add up how much time each one spends doing their particular chores, you'll both end up in a dead heat, 50-50.

Tell you what I'll do. Try it for just a year and keep track of the amount of time you and your mate spend doing chores around the house. If my 50-50 guess is off by more than a paltry 5 percent, I'll personally came over to your home and do the laundry for you.

First, you've got to find me!

Speaking of married people, did you ever notice how married women tend to treat us singles as though we have leprosy or something? I once attended a planning meeting where married and single women were planning a local charitable event. It was very noticeable that most of the married women were just "putting up with" the single women, as if their ideas and opinions weren't really worth listening to. It was so obvious that it was disgusting. I couldn't help but chuckle, however, knowing that in a couple of years the odds are that probably a third of these snobbish women will have joined the ranks of us singles.

Revenge will be sweet!

While ALL women are hard to understand, some are totally impossible. One such woman was a gal I knew in California. I'll call her "Poopsie" (not her real name). Poopsie was a nymphomaniac, and a *creative* one at that. She had had some writing experience, and one day she decided she was going to write a book on the different ways men make love. To facilitate her research on the subject, she ran this ad in the personal section of the local newspaper.

> **MEN WANTED!** Female writer is writing a book on the different ways men make love. Needs young, willing male volunteers over age 21 to discuss/demonstrate. No compensation except anonymous mention in book. Call . . . Saturdays and Sundays, noon to 5:00 p.m.

Poopsie's phone rang off the hook, and demonstration appointments were made fast and furious. In no time her neighbors were up in arms at the number of pick-up trucks lining the streets in front of her apartment, and they eventually forced her to move, but not until she had discussed/demonstrated the different ways men make love with over 70 volunteers.

By the way, Poopsie never did write her book, and I'm not really sure she ever expected to. What I do know is that it will take many years to wipe that smile off of Poopsie's face.

Here's another example of how impossible it is to understand women, at least SOME women. This is another true story, unbelievable as it may seem.

This gal (we'll call her Susie) was about 40-ish and she dated a guy (Sam) who was about 50-ish. They were "weekend" lovers, and while Susie was head-over-heels in love with Sam, he merely was in "lust" with her. She spent many a night in his apartment making "unprotected" love, except during her fertile days of the month, when he would use "protection." Sam would always check with Susie to see whether it was "safe" time or "Trojan" time, as he called it. Even though they made love over an 8-month period, Sam didn't realize that Susie was a very devious person. One night, she figured out how to trap poor Sam for the rest of his miserable life. When she knew that she was in her fertile period, she told Sam that she was "safe," and they set about making unprotected love as they had done hundreds of times before.

Several weeks later, she called Sam and said, "Guess what? I'm pregnant!"

A flabbergasted Sam asked how she could be pregnant, since the last time they made love she had said she was "safe." Susie replied that she had lied. She said she wanted to have Sam's child because she knew that he had been such a good father to his children from his previous marriage and that she was sure he'd treat this new child with the same attention and visit it often. She thought she would be able to see Sam on a regular basis for much of the rest of her life. In other words, she thought she had trapped Sam into a lifelong commitment, even though it was totally against his will. Can you believe that?

Naturally, Sam hit the ceiling and refused to have anything more to do with Susie. As nature would have it, probably because of her advanced childbearing years, Susie miscarried soon thereafter, and Sam was spared. If nature hadn't intervened, Sam would have become a prisoner of his own lust. It's an amazing but true story.

Here's another thing that mystifies me about single women: the number of them who seek out MARRIED MEN for their liaisons. I've talked to some single women who date ONLY married men. I asked one once why she would go out only with married men and she answered very frankly that she likes sex but doesn't want to get involved with a man who might get serious with her. Dating a "happily" married man serves both purposes.

Another single woman, using some real twisted logic, said that the only way to avoid getting Herpes, AIDS, or VD is to date only married men, because they make love to only one woman . . . their wives. She didn't seem to realize that if he is cheating with her, he might be cheating with other women, too. Thus, he's got just as good a chance of catching something and passing it on as do single men—maybe even more so! Single men, with their exposure to lots of women on a daily basis, can pick and choose and be selective in their choice of dates. Married men usually have to sneak around and take whatever comes along.

Sometimes dating a married man can become habit forming. One woman (I'll call her Penny) had a casual affair (if there is such a thing) with a traveling salesman (married, of course) and soon fell head over heels for the guy. She also was married at the time and had a lovely family. When his company relocated him and his family to a city thousands of miles away, she packed up too, left her family, divorced her husband, and followed her lover to his new location, where they both continued their illicit affair, discreetly, right under his wife's nose. Eventually, after nearly 10 years of this double life, he divorced his wife and married Penny.

And they lived happily and suspiciously of each other ever after.

✳ **Dear George:**

I would like to know why there are so many married men out there who don't bother to wear wedding bands. I've heard all the arguments, and none of them wash. Most of us single women can tell a married man with or without his wedding ring. Though we do get fooled occasionally, most of us would not go out with a married man by choice. So when it happens, we're as shocked as anyone. Tell your married and engaged female readers not to blame the "other" woman but to blame themselves and their husbands when something like this happens.

Sounds to me like you've just been hoodwinked by a married man posing as single. Sorry about that! We single men have enough problems finding good, single women. We don't need any more competition.

You can usually spot the married men by the band of pure white skin on their ring finger, where their wedding ring normally is, or by the Band-Aid they wear on this finger to cover up the white band of skin.

You can also detect them very easily because they are the ones who need to "score" right away. They know they don't have much time before their spouses hunt them down and give them hell.

Single men, on the other hand, have all night . . . so to speak!

* 16 *

Women and Dancing

IT SEEMS TO ME that most women would rather dance than eat and that most men, on the other hand, would rather eat than dance. How did we develop this disparity between the sexes? Could it be easily resolved? If we are ever going to understand women, we must first resolve this dilemma.

I took it upon myself to conduct a research survey among women—thousands of women—married and single, to discover why they like to dance so much. I figured that if we men knew the answer to that question, we could adjust our attitudes and, with our newfound understanding of dancing, become better dancing partners.

So I ran an exhaustive survey among the female readers of my singles column and asked them to check off over sixty items of information. I had firmly resolved that once and for all we men would understand and appreciate why women die for dancing. I also asked my married readers to respond, separately. The results follow.

These results will probably reinforce women's feelings about dancing. But they will be a real eye-opener for men like me. As a result of this survey, I developed a whole new outlook on dancing and am now an enjoyable dancing partner—stepping on toes aside.

Of the thousands of replies I received, here are the four most important reasons why women like to dance, in order of importance:

1.   Women love music and would rather share it with a man.
2.   A woman likes her body moving in rhythm with a man's.
3.   Women think dancing is intimate and sexy, and has sexual connotations.
4.   Women feel it is romantic and a part of the courting ritual.

Zounds! I had all kinds of other ideas about what women would have picked, such as hugging and cuddling. And I'm sure that most men would have said that dancing to women was just a brief pause on the way to the sack. These choices finished far out of the money. I'm a "reborn" dancer again. Now all I have to do is relearn how to do it.

As part of this same survey, I asked women of all ages what type of dance they liked the most. This also was a shocker. The most popular form was Latin dancing, followed by slow dancing (foxtrot, two-step, etc.), with swing (jitterbug) in third place, and disco in fourth. A close fifth place went to the waltz.

Another question I asked was what type of person women preferred to dance with. Most prefer a partner who was as tall or taller and, in second place, one who was a good dancer or liked dancing. Next came "good conversationalist" and sense of humor, followed in fourth place by "slim" or in good physical shape.

Armed with this information, I'm sure most of us men will now know how to approach the dance floor with more confidence.

Chiropodists and podiatrists . . . here we come!

* **17** *

Men and Dancing

SINCE THIS IS AN equal opportunity book, it's only fair that we discuss the male gender's attitudes toward terpischorian activity. I'm sure some of the comments I came up with will be just as eye opening to the women as some of their comments were to us men.

* **Dear George:**

I read your column before I do anything else. I noticed where several women had written you complaining about men who sit at a dance and don't ask women to dance. I see it all the time at every dance I attend, even at the dance parties at the studios where I take dancing lessons. What's wrong with you men? Are you afraid of us dainty little women? We're the weaker sex, aren't we?

Weaker sex? Baloney! Anyone who can give birth to a baby and be back on her feet an hour later doesn't sound very weak to me. If men delivered babies, it would take most of us 6 months to recover, and then another 6 months to complain about it.

But as far as men not asking women to dance, I have researched this over the years by quizzing hundreds of nondancing men. When I asked them why they don't dance, I got a lot of really solid reasons. You women, instead of fighting it, should figure out ways to overcome it.

Here are my survey results from nondancing men:

1. **Many (if not most) men are basically shy.** I mentioned this in a previous chapter, and it bears repeating again, since it was the most prevalent reason for not dancing. Many men will NEVER ask to dance a woman to whom they've not been introduced. I know you women refuse to believe it, but this reason tops the list.

2. **Many men lack confidence in their dancing ability.** If a man doesn't feel he is a good dancer, and he sees the dance floor crammed with Fred Astaire–types, he'll be reluctant to dance because he doesn't want to be the worst dancer on the floor.

3. **Many men simply don't like dancing.** But then, you ask, why does he even bother to go to a singles dance if he doesn't like to dance? His answer, "But where's a better place to meet single women than at a singles dance?"

4. **Many men don't like women's attitudes.** The men figure if the woman doesn't look like she cares about dancing—or about dancing with him in particular—why bother to get turned down.

5. **Many men fear rejection.** I don't care who he is and how tough he might be, when a man asks a woman to dance and she says no, to many men this rejection is very painful. It's sort of like having a circumcision at age 50, performed by Doogie Howser, M.D. So, rather than face the possibility of being rejected, a lot of men just won't bother to ask in the first place, unless (and I've said this twice before because it's so important for women to develop) *the woman makes the first move or shows some interest in him.*

6. **He may find the available dancing partners undesirable.** Let's face it. A man doesn't dance because he wants to wear out some shoe leather. He dances because you are attractive to him in one way or another, whether it's your dancing ability, personality, magnetism, looks, figure, inheritance, money, etc. If you don't fit into one of the categories that HE finds desirable, then you are undesirable, *at least to him.* Everyone appreciates different things.

7. **He may be turned off by certain women.** Some people just turn off other people. I remember once when a woman approached me in a local nightspot. She had recognized me and started to bawl the hell out of me, because none of the men in the place had asked her to dance. THIS LADY WAS A REAL TURNOFF, to me and to every guy in the place, and I could quickly understand why. First of all, she sized up all the men as if she were planning to give them an examination, and this turned men off pronto. Her conversation was totally negative and complaining. And when she got close enough, it was obvious that she must have recently fallen into a vat of fresh garlic sauce, as every time she breathed, it melted the hairs in your nostrils. A real turn-off person.

I must say, I was really proud of the men that evening.

Maybe these survey results will allow you women to turn a wallflower into an "Astaire." A good way to get started is to use the "ladies choice" dances that most singles gatherings offer. It's your chance to show the bashful men that you are interested in them, without being pushy. And when you finally drag your Mr. Wonderful onto the dance floor, give him some kind of pleasant compliment to put him at ease. He might just want to come back for more—and you're off and running. But be honest in your compliment. Don't tell him how light he is on his feet after he has just imprinted "Cats Paw" all over your white shoes. A little compliment or reassurance on your part will go a long way toward making him feel comfortable with you. "Ladies choice" dances were invented for one reason—they work!

Why don't you make a concerted effort at the next singles dance you attend to identify the types of men I listed here, and then see what you can do to change them. It should be fun.

✴ **18** ✴

Age and the Age Difference

THIS IS ANOTHER touchy subject . . . but I haven't shied away from touchy subjects so far, and I'm not going to start now.

✴ **Dear George:**

I am 59 years old, fairly well off, and have been dating a gorgeous 32-year-old gal. I've been thinking of taking the plunge and getting married but am concerned about the age difference. What do you think?

If she starts calling you Da-Da, you'll know she's searching for a father image, since you are old enough to be her dad. Twenty years from now, when you're a tired 79, she'll be a lively 52. How are you going to keep her mind off the hordes of younger men who will undoubtedly vie for her attention. I know of several successful marriages between people with greater age disparities than yours, but I know of a lot more that aren't successful. I guess the things to look for are how mature she is and how caring she is, and what lasting attributes YOU possess, other than your money, to keep her interest during your "golden years." Another question to ask is, "Is she in love or looking for security?" There are an awful lot of things to be considered before you plunge into a marriage with this wide age difference.

It might be better if you instead plunged into a cold shower!

✳ **Dear George:**

Why do men in their 50s usually prefer much younger women, instead of a compatible companion for the rest of their lives?

Maybe it's because they don't think the women they know in their own age groups are really compatible for the rest of their lives. Please note the following letter.

✳ **Dear George:**

It sounded like several of your readers thought poorly of a man dating a woman 25 years younger than he. If you haven't tried it, don't knock it! I'm 34 years old, considered quite attractive, and have been dating a man 57. He's not rich, so I'm not a gold digger. But he is caring, considerate, and thoughtful. Every time I go out with him, I learn something new, or we go to a new place. He isn't boisterous, knows his manners, can hold his liquor, and is a perfect gentleman. I'm proud to be seen with him.

Many people still feel that with the age difference between you, sooner or later you're going to stop caring for him—just about the time when he reaches the age when you must start caring for him, if you get my drift.

✳ **Dear George:**

How do you get a guy who is younger than you are to ask you out?

How much younger? Five years? No sweat! Use the same feminine wiles you use to get older men to take you out. But if you are talking about a LOT younger, you'll probably first have to convince him that you both are on the same wavelength and that there isn't a severe generation gap between you. Then follow up with your usual feminine wiles. When all else fails, you still have us old bucks waiting in the wings.

✳ **Dear George:**

Why won't a younger fellow date an older woman? Are they afraid of what society will think of them? I'm an older woman who is still attractive and sexy, but younger men seem scared. I'd be interested in your comments.

I asked a number of men this same question, and here is a brief recap of their comments:

An accountant in his 30s said older women have a tendency to "talk down" to younger men. They've been around more and traveled more and don't hesitate to let the younger man know that they don't think he is up to her caliber of experience and intelligence.

A 40-ish man said older women are too possessive. If you act friendly toward them, they misinterpret it and don't want to let you go. They seem to want to "own" you right away and act insulted if you don't respond in like manner.

One man felt that women age quicker than men do, and a pretty 50 year old today might not look "so good" 5 years down the road. He said there's a certain amount of pride connected with dating.

A yuppie computer programmer said he wouldn't go out with a woman 20 years older than he is because she'd be his mother's age, and he couldn't handle the thought. He did say, however, that he wouldn't mind a woman up to 5 years older than he, provided she was at his level in the things that interested him.

Most men are in the habit of dating younger women because, as we've been told all our lives, women mature much earlier than men. Thus, if the man is 4 or 5 years older than the woman, then they're about equal in maturity levels, so the story goes.

To this I say, BUNK!

I have met women 10 years older than I who don't have the maturity of a mayfly. And I've met many women 10 years younger who are extremely mature. I say that everyone has to be judged according to his or her individual merits, not with a broad brushstroke. The important thing is how two people relate to one another. Are they comfortable with each other? Do they share the same feelings and ideas? Are they compatible? These are the things that make for a happy life, regardless of the ages of the couple.

Speaking personally, I have enjoyed many great times with women older than I, and I didn't find any of the problems these interviewees expressed.

But I've noticed my mail in recent years has carried more and more letters from women wanting to date younger men. What's wrong with us old bucks? We can still do everything the young guys can. We just do it with more finesse . . . and more rest periods.

✳ Dear George:

I've been reading with interest your columns about older women dating younger men. One fellow said to me that men don't date older women because they cost too much. He's not scared; he just can't afford us. But fear not. Most of us grannies would just like a dancing partner or an escort to go places with. Most of us would be happy to go Dutch treat just to have an escort.

I once met a man at a singles party who was in his mid-70s. He had just filed for a divorce from his bride of 4 months. He told me that he had married a 49-year-old woman against the advice of nearly everyone he knew. In this case, it wasn't so much because of the 25-year age difference between the bride and groom. The main reason for the negative advice was that the woman had a 14-year-old son living with her, and a boy that age is too much for a man in his 70s to help raise. But the man wouldn't be deterred. He loved the woman and—son or no son—the wedding went ahead as planned.

Moments after the bride and her son moved into his home, trouble started. He wanted the boy to be raised the same way he had raised his own sons half a century earlier, and he couldn't understand why his advice wasn't followed (and, in fact, was scorned).

The difficulties of coping with a young son ended this marriage before it ever got a chance to start. In this case, the "age difference" skipped a generation, and the marriage was ruined because of the vast age difference between the *man* and the *boy*.

In all my experience interviewing singles who got remarried, the biggest problems encountered in their married lives were associated with raising stepchildren. And if there is a great age disparity between the marriage partners, the problems are even worse. Also, the situation is DOUBLY hazardous if the children's natural father or mother lives nearby and sees the children often, dispensing contrary advice to that given by the new stepparent about how the children should behave. It can become a real nightmare.

✳ **19** ✳

Getting Over Someone

I T SEEMS THAT IT WOULD BE EASIER to get over someone whom you divorced after a bad marriage than it would be to get over a spouse who died. But quite often that doesn't appear to be the case, especially for women—or especially for the thousands of divorced and widowed women I surveyed. Except for a handful of instances, newly divorced women seem to crawl into a shell of self-pity and isolate themselves from the rest of the singles world. They seem to reject single life as a disgusting and distasteful way of life, even though they freely chose this path themselves. According to my survey, newly divorced men feel this to a lesser degree and are quicker to accept their fate than most women.

Widows and widowers, on the other hand, seem to more readily accept getting into the singles swing again. Certainly, they still mourn the loss of their loved ones, but once they face the awful reality that that person will never be around again, they accept the inevitable and socialize much more quickly and heartily. Maybe the reason for the differences between divorced and widowed people is that the divorcees, knowing that the "ex" is still around, may subconsciously hold out hope that they might rekindle the spark that got them together in the first place.

✳ Dear George:

My girlfriend and I broke up 8 months ago, and ever since, I've had empty arms. Because of our separation, I feel I will never be able to love another. How do I overcome this fear of mine? How do I go about finding another after 3 years with the same one? Please help me.

As I mentioned at the beginning of this book, I don't give any psychiatric counseling. You'll have to go to the experts to get that. But I have put together a "getting over someone" formula, expressed in layman's terms, that seems to hit the nail on the head as far as the length of time it takes to get over a busted romance, an unwanted divorce, or the death of a companion whom you really loved. I call it the three phases of love.

PHASE I—I call this simply the "I love you" phase. When you break up or lose a person in this phase, it normally takes 2 weeks to 2 months to get over it and dismiss the person from your daily thoughts. After this time period has elapsed, you quickly move on to your next relationship.

PHASE II—I call this the "I love you a ton" phase. Breaking up in this phase usually takes 2 to 6 months to get over. It's hard to live with, but be patient, it will pass. Continue your life as you had before, except don't frequent those special places that meant so much to the both of you.

PHASE III—I call this the "I can't live without you" phase. When you lose or break up with a person in this phase, you're devastated. You can't sleep at night, and the other person is constantly on your mind, 24 hours a day. You don't care about eating, and when you finally socialize, all you can think about is your ex-lover. Every sad song you hear seems to have been written precisely to describe the feelings you now have. It's total murder but, like everything else, you'll recover. I figure it takes 6 months to 2 years to recover from Phase-III love.

When a marriage or a love affair ends, at first you can't tell what phase you are in because they all seem to hurt equally bad the first week or two. But as the days wear on, you become aware of what phase you're in by how quickly or how slowly you recover; it's sort of an after-the-fact happening. But take heart. Everyone recovers. Time heals all wounds. Just keep yourself as busy as possible during the recovery period.

The letter writer on the previous page seems to be in Phase III. It's hard to end the affair, and it's hard to forget it. Here are a few ideas that have worked for others that I suggested he follow to help endure Phase III until it passes. They work equally well for men and women.

Go out with or chat with as many women as you possibly can, and pay attention to the special "positive" traits that each woman possesses. Only look at the pleasant traits and fill your mind with the best features of each woman. But NEVER compare these women with your ex-girlfriend, since no one can compare or come close to her in your mind, at this time. And by paying attention to the attributes of a lot of different women, it will put something else in your mind besides your ex-girlfriend.

NEVER discuss your ex-girlfriend with any other women. All it will do is solidify her in your mind and make you a crushing bore to the other women. Put your "ex" out of your conversations.

NEVER play a radio station that specializes in country-western music. Every song they play will remind you of your "ex," and all the songs they play will seem as though they were written about the two of you.

Don't keep things around the house that remind you of her. Store them away. It's hard to throw them away right now, but it'll be easier in 2 years.

Don't call or write your "ex" or any member of her family. Make a clean break.

Don't sit home alone on weekends. Join a bowling league, card group, sports team, or some other social activity to keep yourself and your mind occupied. Join a singles group. Attend church regularly and become involved in their activities as much as possible. If you keep yourself overly active, she'll occupy less of your thoughts before you know it. And soon, you'll hardly think of her at all! (See how much trouble you gorgeous gals cause?)

✳ **Dear George:**

I read all of your columns and I really enjoy them. You are always fair to the people who write you. So here goes. How long does it take to get back to where you want a relationship again? I have been divorced long enough that I should want more than something "casual." I have dated several people, and as soon as they start getting close I either stop seeing them or make them so miserable that they stop seeing me. This is not something I do deliberately. I only realize what has happened after it's too late to undo the damage I've done. The difference this time is that I see what I'm doing. I'm pushing away the person I'm seeing. He must think I'm crazy, and I'm beginning to think he's right. How long does it normally take before you learn to trust again? Is there a certain time frame, or does it take a giant step to get your feet wet again?

Join the crowd. It seems to me that most of us (or at least an awful lot of us) just coming off a divorce or broken romance, tend to do the same thing you've been doing, that is, building a wall around ourselves. I guess we all figure subconsciously that we just got through being "burned" and we're not about to let it happen again . . . at least not for a while.

A lot of people I know won't even date a newly divorced person or a newly "free" one; they don't want the bother and hassle of trying to break down the wall that someone else caused to be built. It's easier to wait it out somewhere else with someone else.

One man who was in this same predicament told me he acted basically the same as you have. He was "gun shy." He had recently gotten over a heavy relationship and had just begun to date a new woman, when she wrote him a nice letter—I don't know about what—and signed it, "I'm yours forever." This scared the pants off him to the point that he stopped seeing her. The "wall" he had built around himself was still too high, and he was still nervously hiding behind it. If the woman had waited a little longer until the time was right for him, when she would have sounded less "serious," who knows what might have happened. He says she really might have been HIS FOREVER. I guess all it takes is a little patience, a lot of good timing, and a whole bunch of "wall" dismantling.

✳ **Dear George:**

How long does it take emotional burnout to heal?

It takes about 3 weeks, 4 days, and 3 or 4 hours (depending on your time zone).

I'm just kidding, of course. I presume you are talking about the time it takes to get over someone you really cared about. The time periods in my Phase I, II, and III theory seem to hold pretty much true for just about every one of the thousands of singles I've discussed it with who suffered a busted romance or loss of a loved one.

✳ **Dear George:**

How long should you wait after your husband's death to get out into the world again? My husband died 8 months ago (at age 49) after a lingering illness. Now I want to go to some singles functions, but my friends say it's too soon. They say I should wait a year out of respect for my husband. What do you say?

I say tell your friends to mind their own business. I don't know who came up with that "1 year" bit, but I've heard it many times before. It looks to me like it's more to impress the "living" than it is true respect for a departed loved one. How can you put a time frame on mourning?

I know many people who have mourned the death of a loved one for many years, and that's fine. But many others are ready to start their lives up again much before the year is up, and that's okay, too. In my opinion, it is up to YOU, not some friends who are only interested in appearances. If you're ready to resume living, then get going. It's just as easy to respect a loved one's memory in a group of your peers as it is at home in front of the boob tube.

✳ **Dear George:**

I got through the last few years of a bad marriage by imagining my future with Mr. Wonderful. Now that I am single, I have discovered that even Superman can't hold a candle to the Mr. Wonderful figment I came up with, and I have lost many good friendships because of my fantasy. Is this problem exclusive to me or to women in general?

I presume the reality that there is no perfect human—male or female—has hit you. The Mr. Wonderful you imagined probably will never exist, but at least it served its purpose and helped you through the final years of your rocky marriage. It has done its job, so now put it to rest and begin judging each person on his individual merits, not on some figment of your imagination.

My idea of a perfect Mr. or Ms. Wonderful is someone with whom we agree and approve of 51 percent of the time. Anything over 51 percent, and you've got your Superman.

* 20 *

Singles Pitfalls

As with any course we chart in life, there are potholes and detours that must be encountered and overcome as we journey to our destination. Some pitfalls of single life may be stranger than those of married life. But once we identify them for what they are, we can easily learn to cope with them or ignore them. Pitfalls in single life are really no big deal if we don't make them such.

* Dear George:

Do you have a sure-shot rebuke or answer to a married man making a proposition to you because you are a widow?

That's easy! Take your choice. Tell him one of the following:
1. "I'm an old friend of your wife."
2. "My new boyfriend is an insanely jealous rifle-marksman."
3. "I'll call you when my herpes subsides."
4. "It's okay as long as you bring a letter from your wife."
5. "Bug off you creep!"

* Dear George:

I am a widow and take care of my 82-year-old mother. She doesn't want me to date anyone or go anywhere at all. She resents it. Any answers will help.

I am assuming your mother has her full mental faculties. If so, then my next question is: Who is going to care for you when YOU'RE

82? Judging from the rest of your letter, you've been a very dutiful daughter, and your mother should bless the day she bore you. And she should expect you to live your own life as much as possible. By all means, go out on as many dates as you can. Lord knows good dates are hard enough to find as it is, and if you get a good one, grab him!

Perhaps you can get a neighbor to check on your mother while you're out. And if you are gone for an extended stay, you can usually hire someone to keep an eye on her. You can also install a security system that monitors her well-being. I think most people would say it's best to explain to your mom that you also have a life to live, then go live it. Here's another idea: Why not find an 82-year-old man for her and double date? She might even teach you a thing or two.

✳ **Dear George:**

Since you've run so many singles dances and parties, maybe you can tell us first-time women what kind of men to be wary of.

I've touched on it before, but I'm glad to do it again. On a very few occasions, you'll find con men or just plain "weirdos" stalking a singles get-together, looking for some gullible women who will become their next victims. It could be an investment broker, a sex fiend, or a host of other unsavory types looking for the perfect "target." No one said the singles scene is perfect, nor is the married scene, for that matter.

Here are a few ways to help avoid being victimized by unsavory men at a singles party:

Don't be misled because the guy is handsome, well dressed, or a smooth talker. The best con men in the world are all these and more. Pay attention to what's underneath the facade.

Leave your diamonds and jewelry at home. They'll only attract the unattractive.

Don t be snowed because he s a good dancer. Pay attention to everything else about him. And follow the advice I gave earlier in this book about not giving out telephone numbers and addresses until you KNOW it s okay.

One time when I had published this advice in one of my newspaper columns, a widowed reader evidently forgot about it and soon thereafter met a man who she thought was the answer to a widow s prayers. They went dancing almost every night (he was such a marvelous dancer so light on his feet, she said). He was handsome, polite, slim, and trim, and very well dressed. She showed him off every chance she could to the other single ladies, who were not as fortunate as she. She was totally snowed by the guy and never even bothered to check into his background. You know the rest of the story.

They got married. She bought him a new home. She added his name to her sizable checking and savings accounts, and gave him power of attorney over her securities. She was in love, blindly.

But the love lasted only until she discovered that he was a philanderer, not to mention a heavy drinker. These things were pretty well known to just about everyone else in town, but she went into the relationship with both eyes shut! After all, he was such a marvelous dancer . . . and so polite!

To make a long story short, she lost just about everything she had. She even lost the respect of her single women friends, who were not as fortunate as she.

That s why you ll find me repeating myself when it comes to cautioning women not to rush blindly into an affair until you REALLY know the guy. The waters of single life are teeming with all kinds of piranhas, snakes, and other predators.

However, the alternative of staying home alone night after night without making new friends is even worse. Just do your fishing in calmer waters so that you ll avoid the sharks. And *keep your eyes wide open* (unless you re kissing, of course).

21

Holidays and Anniversaries: Lonely or Happy?

I OFTEN HEAR FROM PEOPLE who think of Christmas (and many other holidays and anniversaries) as a sad and gloomy time of the year. They spend their holidays longing for the days of yore, when they had their families around them. Now with family members gone, and no spouse, the loneliness becomes an extra heavy burden . . . especially during the Christmas season. But it doesn't have to be this way.

Dear George:

I was thinking about how I got through my last two Christmases as a divorcee. I became single after 14 years of marriage, and I keep reminding myself how much better life is today. Sure it used to be nice to have someone there all the time during the holidays, but was it worth the price you paid the other 11 months? Most of us became single by choice, but we tend to remember the good times more clearly than the not-so-good times, and that can result in sadness and regrets. I can truly say that my past two Christmases as a single woman were among my best. There were months when I would have liked to share them with someone special, but I now have choices I can make myself. I know in a few years, when I've got it all together, I'll share it with someone who will make it last 12 months a year, and then I'll have it all.

Sounds to me like you've got it all together right now.

Many psychologists claim that the gloom around the holidays is a result not of longing for days of yore but of shorter days with less sunlight. Too much sun deprivation over a period of time affects our attitudes and can cause depression.

Every Christmas day when I'm alone, I like to dwell on the fun my grown children are having that day, in their homes, with their little ones. The fact that they are enjoying themselves brings me much joy. After all, I raised them to make the most of their lives, and now when they are doing just that, I can sit back and enjoy the fruits of my labors in raising them. Christmas and anniversaries are special times of happiness for me because I choose to look at them with a positive attitude.

I'm not going to tell you that I never look back a little longingly at those good old times, because I do. But I do it in APPRECIATION for the great times I was lucky enough to be part of, not in sadness that they're gone.

I think this kind of positive outlook is the only way to go. Some people are so negative and so down on everything, that they downright hate the approach of Christmas. And some take it to such an extent that they actually become sick (really) over the thought of the holiday season. In my opinion, these people are "sadness hypochondriacs," looking for a reason to be sad and gloomy. I've seen single people who previously had never felt any melancholy during the holidays suddenly dislike Christmas because their friends felt that way, sort of like the blind leading the blind . . . or the "sad" ruining the "happy." I think they need someone to step in and put a stop to it, rather than what I see so often where people seem to encourage this behavior.

I know of a group of elderly widows in the Midwest who get together every Christmas eve for a dinner party at one of their homes. They invite several married couples to join them, along with their children, to round out the generation spread. They enjoy their guests' companionship, of course. But more importantly, they relive Christmas through the eyes of the younger generation who are eagerly anticipating their Christmas bounty just ahead. As a result, these charming ladies thoroughly enjoy their Christmases.

I have heard singles say—after a particularly lonely Christmas period—that they will never go through that loneliness again. Then they make a New Year's resolution to get married before the next Christmas season so that they will have someone to share it with. But what happens if they aren't really ready for marriage or don't find a compatible mate? If that's the case, they'll end up even more miserable, and not just during the holidays. It seems like a pretty crazy idea to me.

Here are my 10 tips for avoiding and overcoming the Christmas season blues. I guarantee if you'll follow just three of these tips, any three, you'll have a thoroughly enjoyable Christmas as a single person.

1. Don't sit home alone in the evenings before Christmas. There are plenty of people out there just like you who are looking for companionship during the holidays, but they can't find you if you're sitting at home.
2. Attend as many singles functions as possible. And when you do, don't sit in the far corner of the room; instead, stay on your feet and mingle where the crowds are. And don't get involved in long conversations with an old friend. It makes it look as though you are already "taken" and discourages new acquaintances from approaching you.
3. Ask your friends, relatives, and neighbors about the Christmas parties they are going to attend and see whether these parties allow them to bring you as a guest. You'll be surprised at how many parties (corporate or otherwise) during the Christmas season are more like open-house events—to which all pleasant people are welcome. And you'll be surprised at how many singles you'll find at these parties.
4. If you have a favorite neighborhood lounge, ask them what time they have set aside for their good customers to congregate for a special Christmas party. It's a great way to meet lots of people.

5. Wherever you go, wish a Merry Christmas to as many singles as you can find. It opens the lines of communication. Ask the person about his or her plans for Christmas day. If the answer is "to spend it alone," suggest that the two of you spend it together in some activity. People are much more in need of companionship during this time of the year, so such a suggestion is not thought of as being "pushy" but merely as being in the "Christmas spirit."

6. Invite a needy family to your home for Christmas eve dinner. After dinner, have the children each unwrap several gifts that you have bought for them. The looks on their faces will make the whole effort extremely rewarding for you. And the planning and purchasing of the gifts and the dinner will have you looking forward to Christmas with joy and anticipation. You'll soon forget you were ever "blue."

7. Contact a nursing home and ask for the name of an elderly person who will be alone on Christmas day. Then make, bake, or buy a gift, wrap it gaily, and bring it to the person and spend some time with him or her on Christmas day. You'll quickly forget that YOU were ever the lonely one.

8. On Christmas eve, attend a midnight service at a church that has a social gathering after the service (many serve coffee, tea, or wine). Usually other singles who are alone at Christmas will also attend these socials, looking for someone else who is alone. A cheery "Merry Christmas" will usually get the conversation ball rolling. While you are there, ask the preacher whether he or she knows of other single persons who will be alone. Chances are the preacher can introduce you to someone in your same situation.

9. Again, look back on past Christmas holidays in a spirit of APPRECIATION for the great times you were lucky enough to be a part of, not in sadness that they are gone.

10. To avoid future lonely Christmas holidays, learn how to meet your Mr. or Ms. Wonderful by applying some of the tactics discussed in this book.

And when it comes to coping with anniversaries, birthdays, or other fond remembrances of former loved ones, it's best to get out with other people to keep yourself busy and take your mind off the good old days. On a week-long singles cruise that I sponsored a while back, I spent much of one evening dancing in the discotheque aboard ship with a very pleasant, well-adjusted lady. She was a widow in her early 50s.

We danced a number of dances and ended the evening with a bottle of champagne on the pool deck. There was no hanky-panky (sorry about that for you readers who thought this was going to be a juicy exposé), and when we retired at 3:00 A.M. or so, we both went to our separate staterooms.

The following day, I encountered my lady friend on deck, and she told me how grateful she was for such a wonderful evening. I started to say that it was *I* who was grateful, but she stopped me. She explained that the previous day had been her late husband's birthday—an occasion they had always shared. She thanked me for helping her focus on the moment instead of on days gone by. It changed her whole attitude, as it proved to her that she could think and plan and prepare for the future, and move forward as a contented single woman.

I have heard from this woman several times (she's remarried now), and she always reminds me of our evening dancing in the discotheque on my singles cruise and how it was the turning point in her life.

How many people do you know who pass by the turning point in their lives without ever noticing it? They needlessly sit at home moping or living in the past. My advice to all you newly single men and women is to stop vegetating and get out among the living. There is plenty to do, and time's a wasting.

Holidays, birthdays, and anniversaries can still be remembered with thoughts of joy, but keep them in perspective. Explore new experiences that will become the foundation of tomorrow's joys. (This is starting to sound like a sermon. If I were sitting astride a horse, you could call it my "sermon on the mount.")

✳ 22 ✳

Miscellaneous

HOW MANY BOOKS have you read in your life in which a chapter is entitled "Miscellaneous"?

Probably none!

Well you have now! I didn't know where to put these last items. But I thought they were interesting or amusing enough to be included in this book—hence, miscellaneous.

✳ **Dear George:**

Do you think Christian singles should engage in sex?

What a loaded question. I suggest you ask your clergyman and whatever answer he gives you, I'll go along with it. However, if your clergyman is a television evangelist, then I want a second opinion.

✳ **Dear George:**

What four animals does every woman want?

A jaguar in the garage, a mink in the closet, a tiger in bed, and a jackass to pay for it all.

It's always nice to receive a letter from an animal lover. Just hope you don't end up with a dog.

✳ **Dear George:**

Here's a poem I made up that you're welcome to use:

With care they tottered down the aisle,

and then their vows were said.
These two who waited for the day
they could afford to wed.
Two can play at this poetry game. Here's my response:
But those who rush to wed too fast,
before they're really certain.
Wind up paying legal fees
at the final curtain.

✳ **Dear George:**

Do senior singles swing as much as the younger ones?

I'm not a senior single yet, so I can't say for certain. And besides, I don't even own a swing. But judging from the letters I get from senior women, they'd sure like to do more things where men are concerned than they do now, and it seems to be directed more toward dancing, conversation, and companionship than "swinging." As we all know by now, the big problem is there aren't enough senior MEN to go around. We've got too many "empty" swings.

✳ **Dear George:**

Even though I'm far from single, I read your column because of your sense of humor. My 5-year-old granddaughter was playing with her doll and said, "She's going to get a husband." I asked how? She looked at me in surprise and said, "You get out of the house and go get one." I thought you'd get a laugh out of that. Lots of women are still waiting for one to knock on the door.

You said it! I must have talked to several thousand singles who seemed to think that Mr. or Ms. Wonderful would come find them and be knocking on their doors. It ain't never going to happen.

✳ **Dear George:**

I thought you'd like to know about a singles club for investors. We attend monthly investment meetings and decide where to spend our $1.25/month dues. So far our returns have exceeded 55 percent, but as *a dating investment it's not so hot. Among our 110 members, there has been only one marriage, that of the club founder and an investor.*

Looks like at least two of the members received "special" dividends. And it looks like the group is certainly adept at picking stocks, though no so adept at picking "b(l)onds."

Which reminds me, I've got a whole mailbag full of letters from widows and divorcees who tried the stock market, with the advice of a "trusted" broker, and got clobbered. Some ended up selling their homes or going broke following the "get-rich-quick" schemes of "trusted" consultants.

One divorcee I heard from really had a good life. She received an alimony check in excess of $50,000 a year and owned a lovely home, free and clear. One day, "such a nice fellow" talked her into investing in the commodities markets. Once she had signed on the dotted line, "Mr. Nice Guy" skipped town with over $100,000 of her money, forcing her to mortgage her home to pay off the contracts she had unwittingly purchased.

Singles! Before you invest your money with *anyone*, get a list of credentials and references a mile long.

No, make that *2 miles long.*

✳ Dear George:

I've been wondering if some sort of singles club could be formed in which we could exchange services. Many of us have to watch our pennies, and when small jobs around the house need doing, I hate to have to call repairmen with their high minimum service charges.

Wouldn't it be good if we could have a list of singles who would help out in return for something they needed? Also, I think it would be much nicer for the quieter ones among us to feel useful and also to have the opportunity to spend a pleasant afternoon meeting a new person.

This letter got me thinking, so I put together a "singles club" with a purpose: singles helping other singles. I put together some ground rules and helped this writer set up her singles club. She now has over one hundred singles donating services to other singles, in exchange for something they might themselves need either right away or some day in the future.

I called the group "SLOBS," for Singles Lending or Bartering Services.

The members may *lend* a service now when the other person needs it but may not require a return service for many months in the future. And since it's a trade-off in services, it is barter in the truest sense of the word. Hence, the acronym SLOBS fits the bill. (A few stodgy people complained about the name I gave it, but most took it good-naturedly, considering the source.)

Word got around about this new club, and within a week after I had printed my ideas and ground rules, clubs were formed in several states. I suggest that those readers who are interested in becoming more active with other singles consider setting up a SLOBS club in their areas. You can run a small ad in the personal column of your local classified newspaper and establish a centrally located place for your first meeting. Here is the set of rules I put together, which you can distribute at your charter meeting.

Rules for SLOBS (Singles Lending or Bartering Services)

1. Only pleasant, trustworthy, noncomplaining, well-adjusted single people will be admitted as SLOBS.
2. The main objective of SLOBS is to help other singles who need our help, regardless of their sex, age, or income level. SLOBS is not intended to be a dating game or a matchmaking ploy.
3. No fees shall be charged and no tipping allowed. The homeowner pays for supplies, if needed, and performs cleanup and other menial chores associated with the job.
4. Major repair jobs will not be performed. Only small, safe jobs that can be easily performed by amateurs are part of this program.
5. SLOBS members should contact other SLOBS members directly and work out the exchanges they need for the chores

they need to have done. All members will be given a list of all other SLOBS names and phone numbers and the type of service they are best qualified to perform.

6. If you need a chore done for you, but the contributing SLOBS member doesn't need your services in return at this time, go ahead and get the chore done now. Then notify the club president of the amount of time it took to get the chore done and the name of the member who did the chore.

7. The club president will maintain a list of debits and credits each SLOB has coming to him or her.

8. Every hour or fraction of an hour worked will count as one unit.

9. If a member lets a SLOBS member help him or her for 2 hours, but isn't immediately able to return a 2-hour favor for this person, he/she then owes the general account 2 units (or hours) of chores, and the person who helped him/her has a 2-unit credit coming. However, in this example, if the homeowner is able to return only a 1-hour favor, the helper will still have a 1-unit credit in his/her account, and the homeowner will still owe the general account 1 unit. The homeowner is responsible for notifying the club president at once of these unit balances due and owed.

10. A helper who has credits in his/her account can redeem these from other SLOBS members, not just the one he or she originally helped.

11. One-hour units count only for time spent working on the job, not travel time to the job or time spent socializing.

12. Helpers can perform their work without the homeowner in attendance, if so desired and agreed to by the homeowner.

13. Jobs should be scheduled at the convenience of the helper.

14. If you don't have a particular SLOBS member you want to call for a job that you need done, call the club president and let him/her give you the names of those who owe the most units to the account pool so that they can work down their accounts.

15. To avoid burdensome travel, you should ask for help from a member who lives closest to your home.

16. Persons who violate the cooperative, trusting, and giving spirit of the SLOBS club will be terminated immediately, regardless of credits they owe or due them.

Obviously, in a group such as this, you have to be very careful that all the members are thoroughly trustworthy, since they will be invited into other members' homes. To facilitate this, I put together an agreement for every member to sign so that the organizer or the people helping out won't be sued for their mistakes or for accidents or any personal harm or injury. I suggest you read the document carefully, with a local attorney, to be sure you have covered all the bases. This example is merely meant to give you an indication of what I have in mind.

SLOBS SINGLES CLUB AGREEMENT

I, the undersigned, agree that I won't hold liable the organizers or the people contributing to the SLOBS program for any damages, injury, harm, accidents, or loss that may be incurred as a result of my inviting these amateur helpers to assist me in the time of my need. I enter this program at my own risk in an attempt to save money that I normally would have to pay a qualified repairperson from a qualified company. Any losses I incur as a result of this program will be borne by me, with no recourse to the organizers or any of the helpers.

Signature_____ Date_____ Witness_____

Each SLOBS member is given a list of the other members' names and addresses and the type of chores they feel they are most proficient in performing. And even though I call it a "singles club" (and you know how unenthused I am about "singles clubs") it really is a loosely knit group of amateur singles helping out other singles in need.

So far, the hundreds of SLOBS out there are helping plenty of people and, in the process, meeting plenty of new singles. And that—singles meeting singles—is really what this book is all about.

You may want to consider starting a group of SLOBS in your town. You don't need any permission or authorization from me. The fact that you spent a few of your hard-earned bucks for this book is good enough for me.

Really Miscellaneous

I couldn't decide where to insert the following two tidbits, so I came up with this subchapter. I probably should have entitled it "Bad Timing," or something like that, because the items deal with some very bad timing on the part of two women.

One woman I heard from had become bored with her marriage—and her husband—after 23 years of marriage and decided to spring the surprise on him that she was in the process of filing for a divorce. Not knowing she had these feelings, he was totally shocked and angered. He immediately changed his last will and testament, and excluded her from all the things he originally had accorded her. Three weeks later, he died of a heart attack! She was left with virtually nothing!

Another woman—I'll call her Darlene—was sick and tired of her husband constantly tinkering in his workshop in the evenings. He worked all day in the world of high-tech computer manufacturing, and when he got home at night, he'd invariably head for his well-equipped workstation to tinker with new ideas and processes that continually poured from his creative mind.

Finally, her friends and neighbors convinced her that she was missing out on the fun things of life by putting up with this tinkerer, and she divorced him for incompatibility.

One year to the day after the divorce, he invented a device that he patented and sold for MILLIONS OF DOLLARS! He doesn't tinker in the evenings anymore. He's too busy wining and dining gorgeous women on his new yacht!

For you married women reading this book (shame on you!) consider your "timing" before you take any drastic measures.

A bird in the hand is worth two in the bush!

(Also, a bird in the hand can result in a very messy hand.)

Fini

I HAVE OFTEN BEEN ASKED what I get out of running singles events or encouraging other singles to get out among themselves and enjoy life. I guess what I get out of it can best be answered by a letter I received from a wonderful woman who had just wedded a great man she met at one of my many singles parties (in a lounge, naturally). I had sent the couple a wedding gift, as I do for the scores of couples who meet and marry as a result of one of my parties, and she wrote this:

Dear George:

The crystal cake plate was beautiful. But you really shouldn't have sent us a gift. After all, you gave us each other. Your presence at the wedding was greatly appreciated because you were the man responsible for bringing us together. Thank you so much, George, for being such a wonderful person. I hope you are rewarded for all you do for other singles by finding someone really special for yourself.

I have received many, many letters similar to this one from happy people who met as a result of my urgings (or is it harangues?) in my newspaper column. Many of these people previously had been "dead in the water." In other words, their lives had become stagnant. But as a result of my bugging them to death, they have discovered that they are attractive, desirable people. They've gotten out and joined the rest of the world.

148

I hope this book accomplishes these same results for you, the reader. No matter who you are, how you look, what size or shape you are, your age range . . . there is someone out there searching for YOU. And I hope that person will be the perfect mate with whom you can enjoy the rest of your life.

So, quoting the 5-year-old granddaughter in the letter from the previous chapter, "Go out and get one!" Mr. or Ms. Wonderful is out there waiting for you.

Make it easy for you and your perfect mate to meet by being there when he or she arrives. You never know when or where it will happen, so be persistent. And above all, be happy! Be positive! And be proud that you are SINGLE AGAIN!

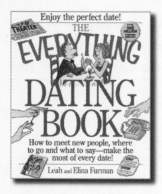

Dating:
A Survival Guide from the Front Lines
Josey Vogels

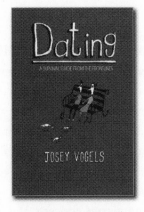

Trade paperback, $9.95
ISBN: 1-58062-176-7

Punchy and provocative, forthright and funny as hell, sex and relationships diva Josey Vogels tells it like it is in this hard-hitting, entertaining and enlightening look at dating in the age of the jaded. From first impressions to first-date foibles, one-liners to one-night stands, Dating delivers savvy tips, lively insight and downright good advice on the often frustrating, but always fascinating, art of coupling.

About the Author

George Blake is a successful advertising executive who suddenly became single after 18 years of marriage. He soon realized how very difficult it was to meet new single acquaintances, so he embarked on a 14-year research program among singles to determine the best ways and the best places to meet other singles. His research involved interviews with over 15 thousand singles from all around the country.

As part of his research, Blake promoted and sponsored over a thousand singles dances and parties, 27 singles ocean cruises, dozens of singles golf and tennis tournaments, numerous concerts and theatre events . . . even supermarket shopping nights.

He started a popular "singles" column for a newspaper chain, which helped considerably with his research. Now the results of his research, along with case histories of how and where singles meet, what they say and do, how they interrelate, and so on, is included in Blake's new book *Single Again* . . . **must** reading for all singles 25 to 80 years of age.